Mercury Rising

MĀNOA 15:1   UNIVERSITY OF HAWAI'I PRESS   HONOLULU

FEATURING

CONTEMPORARY

POETRY

FROM

Mercury Rising

TAIWAN

Frank Stewart

EDITOR

Arthur Sze
Michelle Yeh

FEATURE EDITORS

Photograph by Sergio Goes

Editor   Frank Stewart

Managing Editor   Pat Matsueda

Production Editor   Lavonne Leong

Assistant Production Editor   Jeremy Colvin

Designer and Art Editor   Barbara Pope

Fiction Editor   Ian MacMillan

Poetry and Nonfiction Editor   Frank Stewart

Reviews Editor   Leza Lowitz

Associate Fiction Editor   Susan Bates

Abernethy Fellows   Brent Fujinaka, Georganne Nordstrom

Staff   Charlene Gilmore, Naomi Long, Kathleen Matsueda,
Eryn Nakamura, Leigh Saffold, Amber Stierli

Corresponding Editors for North America
Fred Chappell, T. R. Hummer, Charles Johnson, Maxine Hong Kingston,
Michael Ondaatje, Alberto Ríos, Arthur Sze, Tobias Wolff

Corresponding Editors for Asia and the Pacific
CHINA   Howard Goldblatt, Ding Zuxin
HONG KONG   Shirley Geok-lin Lim
INDONESIA   John H. McGlynn
JAPAN   Masao Miyoshi, Leza Lowitz
KOREA   Kim Uchang, Bruce Fulton
NEW ZEALAND AND SOUTH PACIFIC   Vilsoni Hereniko
PACIFIC LATIN AMERICA   H. E. Francis, James Hoggard
PHILIPPINES   Alfred A. Yuson
WESTERN CANADA   Charlene Gilmore

Advisory Group   Esther K. Arinaga, William H. Hamilton, Joseph O'Mealy, Franklin
S. Odo, Robert Shapard, Marjorie Sinclair

Founded in 1988 by Robert Shapard and Frank Stewart.

Ka-Shue by Lynda Chanwai-Earle, reprinted from The Women's Play Press edition of *Ka-Shue*
(Letters Home), 1998, by permission of the author. Steve Bradbury's translations of Hung Hung's
"A Hymn to Hualian" and "The Last Supper" originally appeared in *The Chinese Pen* (Taipei),
and are reprinted by permission of the translator. "The Legend" by Chu Van, "The End of a Sea-
son of Beauty" by Nguyen Ngoc Tu, "Starting Out" by Phan Trieu Hai, "Thuong" by Phan Thi
Vang Anh, printed simultaneously with *Love After War: Contemporary Fiction from Viet Nam*,
edited by Wayne Karlin and Ho Anh Thai, published by Curbstone Press, by permission of the
translators. The poems by Hsia Yü originally appeared in *Fusion Kitsch*, translated by Steve Brad-
bury, Brookline: Zephyr Press, 2001, and are reprinted by permission of the translator.

Mānoa is published twice a year. Subscriptions: U.S.A. and Canada—individuals $22 one year,
$40 two years; institutions $40 one year, $72 two years. Subscriptions: other countries—individu-
als $25 one year, $45 two years; institutions $40 one year, $72 two years; for air mail add $24 per
year. Single copies: U.S.A. and Canada—$20; other countries—$20. Call toll free 1-888-UHPRESS.
We accept checks, money orders, VISA, or MasterCard, payable to University of Hawai'i Press,
2840 Kolowalu Street, Honolulu, HI 96822, U.S.A. Claims for issues not received will be honored
until 180 days past the date of publication; thereafter, the single-copy rate will be charged.

Manuscripts may be sent to *Mānoa*, English Department, University of Hawai'i, Honolulu, HI
96822. Please include self-addressed, stamped envelope for return of manuscript or for our reply.

www.hawaii.edu/mjournal/
www.uhpress.hawaii.edu/journals/manoa/

CONTENTS

Special Focus ✳ **Contemporary Poetry from Taiwan**

Editor's Note

Mercury Rising is the latest in the *Mānoa* series featuring contemporary literature from Asia, the Pacific, and the Americas. This volume presents new poetry from Taiwan, edited by Arthur Sze and Michelle Yeh, along with work from Viet Nam, the Philippines, New Zealand, Japan, and the United States.

The title *Mercury Rising* alludes to "The Mercury That We Raised So Carefully," a poem by Taiwan poet Hsia Yü that was translated by Andrea Lingenfelter and published in the anthology *Frontier Taiwan*:

> crossing
> black ruined swings
> seeping out from the borders
> a drawn-out dance
> pressing near the antechamber of the flesh
> at six in the morning
> a faint moon comes out

Surrealistic, elusive, international in its sensibility, Yü's poem presents a nearly ego-less perspective in a world simultaneously interior and exterior. A "drawn-out dance" glides across borders, lingers in the rooms inside the body; a silvery moon spills its light into the dawn. A tranquil image, and yet in the rising, mercury-colored moon there is latent instability: when dropped, mercury spills into a thousand copies of itself. How frangible, then, is that moon with its paradoxical essences—perhaps like Taiwan itself, with its unity an amalgam of many parts. In recent years, cultural and political developments have transformed Taiwan from an authoritarian Cold War fortress into a vigorous democratic society where indigenous, immigrant, and worldwide influences freely glide across borders.

For many Western readers, it may seem surprising that such startlingly avant-garde poetry is being produced in Taiwan, a small island a hundred miles off the coast of mainland China. But then, most Westerners know very little about Taiwan's tumultuous history.

The first inhabitants of Taiwan migrated from the Asian mainland, Melanesia, Polynesia, and Southeast Asia more than ten thousand years ago. The government of Taiwan now officially recognizes eleven indigenous groups that, over the centuries, have managed to remain distinct in language, customs, arts, and folklore.

Substantial numbers of immigrants began arriving from mainland China between the eleventh and seventeenth centuries. Eventually, they overwhelmed the aboriginal populations and drove them from the fertile lowlands into the mountains, where they were physically and figuratively marginalized. Present-day Taiwanese social policy is to preserve indigenous language and culture; however, contemporary aborigine poets—such as Monaneng and Walis Nokan, whose work is included in *Mercury Rising*—describe the difficult choices that still have to be made between the traditional and the new. In a poem translated by John Balcom, Monaneng writes:

> If you're an aborigine
> Then wipe away your tears and blood
> And like a huge burning tree
> Light the road ahead.

Indigenous residents comprise only about two percent of Taiwan's population of twenty-three million. The vast majority of Taiwan's citizens are descendants of Han Chinese who were recruited by the Dutch East Indies Company to work on colonial sugar plantations in the seventeeth century. Primarily from Guangdong and Fujian Provinces, many of these immigrants intermarried with aborigine people and made Taiwan their home, even after the Dutch were driven out in 1662. They recognized that Taiwan was a frontier far from the Manchu capital, and they developed a strong sense of independence, by and large resisting control by the central government in China for two centuries.

In 1887, in an attempt to forestall Japanese expansionism, China reasserted jurisdiction over Taiwan. When the Chinese were defeated in the Sino-Japanese War, however, China was forced to cede Taiwan to Japan, without the consent of the Taiwanese people. For half a century, the Japanese attempted to assimilate the island. Taiwanese were forced to take Japanese names, adopt the Japanese language and culture, and even practice Shintoism and worship the emperor.

After Japan's defeat in World War II, the Allied forces granted sovereignty over Taiwan to the Nationalist Chinese party, led by Chiang Kaishek. Taiwan became a military garrison from which the Nationalists waged civil war against the Communist forces of Mao Tse-tung, antagonizing the Taiwanese. Large-scale demonstrations were held, resulting in the massacre and imprisonment of thousands of Taiwanese protestors by the Nationalists.

In 1949, when Chiang Kai-shek's army was defeated, two million people fled from mainland China to Taiwan, the Nationalist government declared martial law, and the "mainlanders" took control of Taiwan's political system, holding power for the next fifty years. In the historic elections of March 2000, the Nationalist Party was defeated at the polls for the first time by the opposition Democratic Progressive Party.

Out of this turbulent past, an astonishingly dynamic literature has emerged. At their best, Taiwan's poets synthesize nativist and cosmopolitan, Asian and European, ancient and avant garde—and they have consciously created a literary climate in which cohesion and difference are not in opposition.

Mercury Rising includes other works in which ideas fuse and flow like mercury. Cuban American poet Ricardo Pau-Llosa, in Alberto Milián's interview in this volume, verbalizes the paradoxes and mercurial existence common to many immigrants, especially those forced from their homeland. "Every exile knows his place," the poet says, "and that place is the imagination."

Lynda Chanwai-Earle, a New Zealand writer and actress of Chinese and European ancestry, imagines the voices and experiences of three generations of women in her play *Ka-Shue (Letters Home)*, printed here in its entirety. The women attempt to understand one another across time and tradition, driven by the forces of history and politics. In "The Cargo," a short story by Filipino writer Anthony L. Tan, the sole survivor of a mass murder contemplates his place in his village's web of relationships. Adrift on a boat, Tan's protagonist tries to imagine a course of action that will require him to neither abandon his village nor return to it.

Four Vietnamese stories are also included in *Mercury Rising*. Chu Van's "The Legend" tells the larger-than-life story of the reunion of a singer and her husband, an officer in the Vietnamese army, during the American War. "The End of a Season of Beauty" by Nguyen Ngoc Tu weaves together two forms of devotion: those of an aging actress to her art and of the man who has loved her for decades despite her rejection of him. In "Starting Out" by Phan Trieu Hai, a young man is caught in the degraded circumstances of city life. "Thuong" by Phan Thi Vang Anh describes the predicament of a modern, free-spirited woman and the three generations of men who desire her.

The three surrealistic, linked stories of well-known Japanese writer Kurahashi Yumiko present a porous reality in which the mundane world is suffused with history, literature, and dream. The characters in Kurahashi's stories pass in and out of history and myth as easily as they step on to a jumbo jet.

At the center of *Mercury Rising* is a portfolio of photographs of the members of Hawai'i's Iona Contemporary Dance Theatre. In these ethereal black-and-white images, photographer Sergio Goes captures the company's signature work, *The Mythology of Angels,* performed in hospices, prisons, and other unexpected settings. In his introduction and lyrical captions, writer Gavan Daws calls the dancers "silvered flesh rising to spirit."

Readers who have been with *Mānoa* for many years will remember the presence of Darlaine Māhealani Dudoit in its pages. The author of many fine works and the editor of *'Ōiwi,* the first native Hawaiian literary journal, Māhealani passed away in August 2002. "Still Center," a poem in *Mercury Rising,* pays tribute to the memory of this warm and vital Hawaiian writer.

The Legend

All of a sudden, every provincial big shot decided to be a poet. The desire to write poetry spread from the highest levels down to the provinces, even the districts. Everywhere they went, provincial and district officials would read their poems aloud and ask the audience for warm applause. The audience would give them a standing ovation. So it was they all became well-known poets.

If the matter had only gone that far, it wouldn't be of any concern. But whenever the big-shot provincial and district officials wrote their poems, a number of flatterers would vie with each other to praise the poets to the heavens. The competitiveness caused much suffering. One day, the flatterers said, "But it isn't enough to have good poems. They should be sung by a female whose melodious voice will seduce the listeners." They cited Tran Thi Tuyet and Chau Loan as examples of those whose sweet voices had immortalized various poets over the air waves.

This advice was immediately taken to heart by one of the province-level poets. Each time he had to attend a conference, he would send his secretary to the office for cultural affairs to request a singer to memorize his poetry and a guitar player to accompany her. These two would join the official and together give a poetry recital. They would be warmly welcomed and given gifts when they left. The quality of the big shot's poems was never questioned. Meanwhile, the district-level poets could only find amateur singers with mediocre voices from the towns or communes in their districts. These poets would travel around in groups, like the clans of singing beggars who set up in village markets.

The poetry disease was like a drug addiction. My elder brother, who was called *cu cop* (Old Bigwig), became seriously hooked. Once, he succeeded in composing a *luc bat* poem (a traditional form with alternating six- and eight-foot verses) and immediately sent his private secretary to summon the chief of cultural affairs, saying he wanted his opinion. On hearing this, the department head grew so afraid that he vanished into thin air, so his deputy went instead. The poet received him solemnly and offered him Chinese cigarettes and green tea. Finally, my brother put on his spectacles and read his poem. It must have been quite melodious because the deputy had to keep pinching his leg to keep from falling asleep. Yet as soon as the reading was concluded, the deputy hunched his shoulders and praised the poem for the high level of its ideological content, its realism, and its beautiful concepts and phrasing. After great depths and breadths of praise, he went on to say that if my brother had been unsuccessful in his official position, he could have been admitted to the Viet Nam Writers' Association and by now would surely be secretary general of that organization.

At that point, feeling he had paid sufficiently for his cup of tea and few fragrant cigarettes, the deputy was ready to leave. But the poet motioned him to sit down, and then told him that since the poem had been so well appreciated, he would have it read at the next conference of the three Delta provinces. He wanted the deputy to take the poem and coerce the female singer Ngan Hoa to learn it by heart and recite it before the conference—without the omission of one period or one comma!

At first the deputy chief was upset by the order, but soon he thought of a way he could use it to get himself promoted. He knew that the head of the cultural affairs office was obstinate toward his superiors and arrogant toward his inferiors. He never engaged in flattery and often poked fun at bad poetry. If all went according to the deputy's plan, his boss would soon be disgraced. Once he's out, thought the deputy, who else but me can become the new chief?

He summoned Ngan Hoa to his office and gave her his instructions. As soon as she heard what she had to do, the singer burst into tears. "What a terrible fate!" She had been about to go home on leave. Her husband was in an air-defense unit and always on the move. They had been married for only a year now and had scarcely had any time together. He'd recently written a letter to her, promising he would request a few days' leave. While his unit was on the march, he would return home to be with her—if not for one night, then at least for a few hours.

Oh! How sacred was this rendezvous! She had already packed to go home, and now, suddenly, she was hit with this bad news. The deputy both threatened and soothed her. "Listen—I'll go to the province chief and discuss your case. But you know he'll just say to tell you to overcome all obstacles and always be on the offensive. There's no use refusing. Doing so would affect both you and the entire office."

He then added, "Listen, I'll ask the province central committee to have a command car take you home. Forty-seven kilometers and two ferries are not such a big journey. Once you're there, you can practice the poem while you're waiting for your husband. When he gets back, take whatever time you need with him, enjoy yourselves. When it's time for the conference, I'll send the command car again, and then after the performance, I'll have it take you back, and you can stay until your leave expires. What are a few hundred liters of gasoline anyway? The province central committee has plenty of it!"

Ngan Hoa was still doubtful. "What happens if my husband comes home right on the day of the conference?"

"No problem—I'll have the car take both of you to the province guest house, where you can have some privacy."

Given those conditions, there was no way she could refuse. Ngan Hoa picked up the poem, put it in her handbag, and went home. Though she wasn't a senior official, she was driven right up to the gate of her house in an official's car, the horn blasting noisily. The commune's cadres, assuming a high official had come to inspect the commune, hurried to greet the car, and were angered to see Ngan Hoa instead.

It was her moment of glory! But for such moments, there is always a price.

At home, Ngan Hoa's mother doted on her. She made her daughter *banh duc* with shrimp paste and pampered her as though she were a young hen awaiting the arrival of her rooster.

She rested for a day, for five days, and then six. Her leave was almost up, but still her man hadn't returned. At first she longed for him, then she lost her temper, and finally she almost went mad. She was exhausted by waiting and longing.

The American planes were bombing many areas. She could hear the roar of the jets overhead, and at night she could see the blue flares rising. She wondered how in the world a lieutenant in charge of an anti-aircraft unit would have time to come home and visit his wife.

Then one evening, early in the month, she looked outside to see headlights flashing and a horn blaring at her mother's gate. In the darkness, she could barely make out the car, which was painted a dark green. It had traveled forty-seven kilometers and had ridden two ferries to collect her. It had barely stopped when the deputy opened the door and stepped into the yard.

"Good evening, *Cu*," the deputy said. "Good evening to everyone. Good evening to you, Ngan Hoa. So where is your husband? Let him come out and have a smoke."

Ngan Hoa sobbed, "He's nowhere to be seen. I had to wait so long, but it was useless."

The deputy chief clucked sympathetically. "Is that so? Well, in the end, it's all the fault of the American aggressors! To miss each other is quite natural for a young couple. Under these circumstances, you have to demonstrate understanding and patience. But tonight you'll have to come with me immediately to the province committee—the conference is tomorrow."

Ngan Hoa knew too well her boss's character, his reputation for being rigid. If she refused to go now, he would make things exceedingly difficult for her. But how tragic to leave now, after she had waited so long. What if her husband returned right after she left? "Can't you make an exception and let me wait until tomorrow morning?"

The deputy didn't say a word. His face darkened. Then the driver piped up, squirming nervously in his seat. "My dear, traveling in full daylight would be very dangerous. The ferries are prime targets for the Americans, and they attack them aggressively. If you have to travel, you have to go at night."

Ngan Hoa's family continued to plead her case, but it did no good. She had to leave then. No matter what the cost. She would be at the conference, and she would recite the poem. Afterwards, the car could take her back, if her husband had returned by then.

The emotional parting lasted for several hours. Finally, though, Ngan Hoa had to wipe away her tears and get into the car. She bore herself like a hostage being sent to a foreign land as a tribute. Meanwhile, the deputy, not a very brave man, sat fidgeting in the front seat. He was so worried about enemy planes that he kept warning the driver, "Be careful. Be very careful." Under his breath, he cursed his boss and the man's infatuation with poetry. "Damn him. What a mess for a few half-awkward, half-idiotic lines of *luc bat*. What if a bomb drops on us?"

As the car bumped along, he could hear Ngan Hoa sobbing at times, and he felt a pang of remorse. But what could he do? He had made his promises; he had to press ahead.

The car drove slowly through the night along the dangerous road. It took more than two hours to get to the Luc Sam ferry. It was late at night, and traffic was clogged, but there were only two ferries. The river here was narrow, but the current very swift. Working without lamps, the youth brigade girls and the workers at the barricades barked orders through loudspeakers: "Drivers are requested to keep order! Don't bunch up!"

The ferry was already packed with cars waiting to cross the river. The yellow circles of their headlights shone in the night. A variety of bicycles and three-wheeled carts surrounded the stubborn and aggressive mechanical vehicles. Drivers swore at each other. Several command cars in the queue carried bigwigs armed with priority orders, but the other vehicles didn't budge an inch for them.

Ngan Hoa was crying. The deputy was wide-eyed with rage, fear, and confusion. The driver was cursing and pressing his horn.

Suddenly, everyone heard the roar of enemy aircraft. In the distance they saw flares bursting against the night sky. The whole noisy, ferocious, incorrigible mob, reeking of sweat and covered with dust, dissolved immediately in all four directions, as though fleeing the hand of death. Within minutes, everything fell quiet. The entire mass of vehicles and people had dispersed, either by finding a place to hide or simply fleeing. With its lights off, the ferry was hidden.

The deputy's car was driven to the corner of a nearby rice field. The driver and the deputy ran for cover. Ngan Hoa quickly climbed out and began running along the path. Her conical hat fell over her eyes. Suddenly, she was startled by a shout: "Who's that over there?! Get down—do you want to die?!"

She fell on her back and managed to get the hat off and throw it away. The distant light of the flare lit the face of the man who had just yelled at her. He appeared a mass of leaves standing on two feet. A cap. Two big eyes. Two hands, gripping a rucksack. A soldier, scared, seeking shelter.

Ngan Hoa screamed as if she'd just received an electric shock. "*Lan!*" She clambered to her feet. As her husband recognized her, he quickly grabbed her around the waist and ran with her toward a deserted area nearby. Breathless, he gasped, "*Hoa!* Why are you here?!" After she uttered a few short sentences, he understood the situation. Ngan Hoa clasped his neck.

"How were you getting home?" she asked.

"My unit is about twenty kilometers from here. I borrowed a bike and started out earlier this evening. As soon as I'd ridden the ferry, the air-raid alarm sounded. I just threw the bike down and started to run."

Ngan Hoa hugged him, shaking uncontrollably. "Go find the bike! Take me home. Go at once, my darling!" Her body was trembling, her eyes filling with tears.

Lan glanced over at the ferry. Everything was quiet, lit only by the flares. He made some rapid calculations in his head: the time it would take to get home and then back to his unit the next day. Finally, the impatient but resourceful soldier came up with a solution.

He searched the area around them with his eyes. Nearby he spotted what seemed to be the floor of a destroyed house and, next to it, a lonely areca tree, its splintered top pointing to the heavens. Without a word, he lifted Ngan Hoa in his arms and rushed toward the tree. Hardly had she gotten her feet on the ground again when she felt him urgently pressing her body against the trunk of the tree. He extracted a flare parachute from his pack and wrapped it around her. As soon as it was draped around her body, she tore off her clothes and tossed them to the ground. In the blink of an eye, there was a naked Eve inside that thin and transparent covering and, as Lan stripped off his uniform and its camouflaging leaves, he became an Adam.

The innocent, slender areca shook and trembled as if molested by a sudden storm. The miserable tree twisted and turned, bent to the east, leaned to the west, assaulted by the two human bodies making passionate love against its trunk. The cocoon of the parachute slammed again and again into the tree, as if trying to beat itself to death. The couple's breathless cries burst from them like gusts from a bellows.

The bombing went on and on. In the sky, the planes continued to swoop down. The flares illuminated everything.

Finally, fed up with hiding, drivers began boldly to leave their cover and run in different directions. The packed bikes and carts moved away until all was clear.

The deputy's driver started the engine and repeatedly pressed the horn. The deputy appeared from his hideout and urged the driver to race to the ferry. But at some distance from them, the areca tree was still shaking, ignoring the flares, the planes, and the all-clear gong. Finally, after a few fierce fits, the areca came to a standstill, as if it had fainted. Two bodies, exhausted and covered with sweat, crept out of the parachute. Only then did they hear the blasting horn.

"Oh God, where's my bike?" Lan asked.

Luckily, both it and his rucksack were still there. "I have to go," he muttered.

"And I have to go also," Ngan Hoa said. "This is what it means to be lovers in time of war. Damn the Americans."

Lan hugged Ngan Hoa tightly. He turned to leave, then turned back, cupped her face and kissed her again. Finally, they ran off in different directions.

To be sure, Ngan Hoa was warmly welcomed at the conference of the three Delta provinces. Of course, everyone thought the *cu cop*'s poem was very good. The singer's voice imbued it with life and with optimism and with love.

Like other epidemics, the poetry infatuation raged for a time and then waned. But the *cu cop*'s poem became the object of literary envy. For certainly, no poet could have created such a mythical love story.

A beautiful child was born from the accidental meeting of the two lovers. That child has now grown up. In their leisure time, all of the old cronies, including the deputy, speculate: "That child could certainly become an artist, because he was conceived at such an original moment. He could become a wonderful dancer because his parents danced an especially magical dance with their four iron feet. He could become a writer because he represents all seven human emotions: joy, sorrow, anger, fear, love, hate, and desire. He embodies magnificent art, fierce days, and a great love!"

Translation by Nam Son and Wayne Karlin

The End of a Season of Beauty

Old Chin always maintained that selling lottery tickets was a matter of some significance. It gave man hope and, if he won, brought wealth to him. But what was of the utmost personal significance to Chin was that his wandering about selling such tickets helped him find the *cai luong* opera singer Hong.

Chin had followed Hong down three streets as she walked with a load of sweetened porridge on her shoulders. They were both in their late sixties now, so their eyesight wasn't good enough for them to recognize each other after forty-six years of separation. But he had remembered her voice, and it sprang from her shriveled lips clear and strong as a song as she called out her wares. Chin was stunned to see her. Her beauty was gone, and her once high neck was bent under the burdens of life. Catching up, he called out, "Miss Hong!" Tears filled his eyes.

He took her hands and invited her to come to the Buoi Chieu [Late Afternoon] House. She wanted to gather some of her belongings first, but he said, "Forget them." Her belongings were nothing but some sweetened porridge and the tattered shack she had erected near a water-fern pond at the end of a lane.

The Buoi Chieu House stood at the end of Cay Cong alley. It was a dead-end street, and only old people lived in the house: the abode of once-famous artists from the reform or classical theater. Chin Vu was a nobody in that artistic circle, but he had helped to found the Buoi Chieu House and, in fact, had named it himself. When asked why he hadn't called it the more likely Hoang Hon [Sunset] or Chang Vang [Twilight] or something like that, he explained that *buoi chieu* meant that there was still some daylight left: these artists still had a role to play in the affairs of society. The Buoi Chieu House was poor, and its expenses had to be covered either by the district or by good-hearted patrons. More vegetables than meat were served in the meals, but all its residents were happy because before they had come to this place, they had led miserable lives, poor as mice. Virtually all of them had been homeless. Some of them had lived in pagodas, some in public gardens or parks; some had wandered aimlessly on the streets.

Coming together in the Buoi Chieu House gave them a chance to sing for an audience again. After all, they were artists.

Chin had taken to selling lottery tickets in order to make ends meet, but he also felt that it was a way to trace friends who were still wandering. After she moved in, Hong continued selling her sweetened porridge; she insisted on it despite the pity everyone had for her. "Let me do it. Chin and I are still young and strong enough…" It was true; they were young compared to the others in the house: he was seventy and she sixty-four. Each morning, Chin shouldered the load of sweetened porridge to the beginning of the alley and then stopped at the base of the *cong* tree, a tree old as a hill—so old it had stopped blooming. He would hand over the shoulder pole to Hong and stand, at a loss for words, until she was out of his sight and he could only hear her sweet voice ringing out in the early morning. Then he would stop at the Tu Bung Café and order a cup of tea.

Once, when someone asked him why he didn't drink coffee, he smiled and shook his head. "I'm saving up to buy a bottle of perfume for her."

At the old man's words, the whole café burst out in laughter. "The geezer is still in love!" someone exclaimed.

"I am," he said, "and there's nothing I can do about it. How could you understand? Ours is an old love story, and I love her even if she doesn't reciprocate."

He finished his tea and stood up. Turning, he addressed the café. "Please come and enjoy our performance tonight."

"What's the name of the play?"

"The Courtship of General Lu Bo and the Courtesan Dieu Thuyen."

"No—you guys did that already. Please sing us 'Nua Doi Huong Phan' [Half of the Beauty's Life], OK?"

"If you wish, but I don't remember the words."

"No wonder, uncle," someone teased. "You always played either a soldier or a servant. You never got to sing a song, remember?"

The old man laughed and turned, snorting ironically. His bent back slowly faded from view.

The residents of the alley were not art lovers, but none of them could forget the singing they heard at the Buoi Chieu House. Even though the singers were well advanced in age, their voices were still sweet. The stage overlooked a large, empty lot. The orchestra consisted of a guitar and an old two-chord fiddle. Without a microphone, the artists would sing with voices blessed by nature. Actress Phi was eighty-nine and unable to stand. She sat on a chair and performed her role, her hand waving a whip. Once, she sang out of tune and cried out, "I can't live like this anymore!"

The people in the alley laughed. "You've lived so long now, what do you have to complain about?"

Since Old Chin couldn't sing, he bustled around, arranging the chair for the actress Phi, rushing in to change a light bulb, and so on. It was only when Hong began to sing that he hid himself and remained silent, missing her even as he looked at her.

He had met her when she was only twenty-one. If people asked him now how he felt about severing his connections to his family, he would just smile at them, as if he regretted nothing. It was well known that he came from a very rich family in Bac Lieu, that he had been their pampered and privileged son. A kind-hearted and generous youth, he had once arranged for the visit of a Saigon drama troupe to enhance the village festival. Hong had been in that troupe. It was the first time he saw her, and he immediately fell in love. He couldn't help it; she was so beautiful she made every man's heart beat faster. When they first met, she had barely finished drinking her tea when Chin burst out, "Have you found someone to marry?"

Hong smiled. "I have sworn before the altar of my ancestors that I will devote myself to my art until my last breath."

Chin Vu hadn't said anything, but had looked at her thoughtfully. The next day, when the Kim Tieu drama troupe returned to Saigon, he left his home and followed them. But he had a rough-looking appearance and couldn't sing, so he wasn't able to perform with the others. His only acting duty was to play the role of a soldier or servant or to reply "yes" or "no" from behind the curtain. In fact, he worked day and night pulling the curtain and getting the stage props set up. He was prepared to work even harder as long as he could see Hong. He often said that the founder of the form of theatrical art known as *cai luong* had cast a spell on him, and he was like the three legendary princes Can, Chon, and Chat, who had abandoned their luxurious court lives to pursue art. Whenever people heard this explanation, they laughed: it was ridiculous to think that a fellow like Chin could be lured by the art of the theater; no, it was clear he must have been struck by love. When he thought about his situation, he considered the possibility that he owed Hong a great debt from a former life—a debt he could not pay in full during this life, no matter how great his efforts.

When Hong became pregnant and the troupe's manager threatened to fire her, Chin pleaded her case. "She is still rather naive, please…"

"Is it yours?" the boss had asked.

Chin smiled. "Yes. No one else's."

"Are you sure of that?"

Yes, he said, his heart filled with sadness. He knew who the real father was, but Hong had begged him not to tell. "Please don't. He still has something very important to do." He knew she must have loved the man very much to protect him at such cost to herself. After she had given birth, Chin took care of the child. When Hong found that he had taught the little boy to call him Ba [Father], she couldn't help crying. It was the first and only reward she'd given him during the two years he'd been with the troupe.

Saigon in those days was in the turmoil of the war, and Chin found himself arrested one afternoon, when the police received information that some members of the Kim Tieu troupe were Viet Cong. All of the members of the troupe were screened, but Chin's background made him suspect. He merely smiled at his interrogators when they asked him why he had abandoned his good life to join the wandering actors. He knew they would not believe the truth. Ten days later, after failing to find any evidence, they freed Chin. Only ten days, but it took him half a lifetime to meet Hong again.

The troupe had disintegrated very quickly, and Hong hadn't waited for him. Later, Chin learned that the actor Thuong Khanh had been arrested by the military police and that Hong had taken her child and gone into hiding, fearing that Khanh, her lover, would falter in his duty if the police used her and the child's safety as leverage against him. Chin searched for her in vain. For years, he wondered how she was able to sustain herself without his support.

One night, Hong told the residents of Buoi Chieu House her life story. They sat in the moonlight, next to a basket of boiled sweet potatoes. Not one person could hold back tears, hearing their own miserable destinies reflected in her story. She had remained true to her vow, staying single for the sake of her art, even though her own son eventually rejected her because of her insistence on following her calling. She never mentioned his name again, in all her life. Chin sat silently, listening in misery. The sadness of her life had taken its toll on her, but he was still struck dumb by her fading beauty.

At Buoi Chieu, Hong became the only female actor never to go on stage without makeup. During her first days there, she had only shaken her head when asked to sing. She never responded to the questions rained on her as a result. All seven women in the house were old and couldn't afford lipstick. When Chin insisted, she told him the truth. He immediately broke into his savings and bought her lipstick and face powder. Hong was moved, but also very sad.

"Why are you so good to me?"

Her words made Chin sad as well.

"Why can't you understand me, even at our age? Oh, my dear Hong."

But he wasn't being completely fair. There were times when he didn't understand her as well. Hong had an old, dull, bronze-edged mirror she liked to use. Somehow this made Chin love her all the more, and he bought her a new mirror and then hid the old one. She became very angry with him. "Don't be so clever. I don't need a new mirror."

"But it's very old, very dull."

"I like it, in spite of its dullness."

He never understood why she preferred the old mirror.

He was sad that day. He did not go to greet her when she came back. He knew she was still waiting for something in her life, but he did not know what it was, nor did she confide in him. She had always been an introvert, always kept her face expressionless and hid her emotions. It was only on stage that she could cry her heart out or laugh to her heart's content.

One day, when all the other residents of Buoi Chieu were picked up and taken by bus to the municipal theater for a commemoration of the death of the founder of the classical theater, Chin stayed back to look after the house. While he was there, an old man with snow-white hair, a deliberate gait, and a very respectable bearing came to the door and inquired after Hong. Chin asked him how he knew her.

"She and I were old friends. Have you known her for a long time? Yes? So you know. How can anyone forget such beauty? I recently read a story about this place. I felt as if I'd been given a second chance at life, and I rushed here to find her."

Chin was at a loss. The man left, with Chin giving no sign that he knew who he was. Thuong Khanh was very old now, but he still had a refined and deliberate bearing. Chin had waited for him to mention the son he had had with Hong. Could he forget so easily? Chin thought about it for a long time before deciding not to tell Hong about the visit. He feared he would lose her again.

But he couldn't remain silent. "Hong, do you remember Thuong Khanh? He came looking for you today."

Hong stopped combing her hair, but she said nothing. Then she went to wash her clothes. At the water tank, she gazed at her reflection and burst into tears. Her faded beauty. Without turning her head, she knew that Chin had come running up to see what was wrong.

"If he comes tomorrow," she said, "please tell him that I don't live here… I don't want to see him again."

At that, Chin felt happy. But he also pitied her.

"Dear, you can't avoid meeting him; there's no use trying. We exist because we have hearts."

One day soon after, Khanh was waiting at the head of the alley. Hong returned home at twilight and spotted him first. She smiled. "I heard that you've been looking for me. Is that true?"

Khanh stood dumbfounded, pain rising in his heart. This was not the beauty he had loved. This could not be Hong, the woman whom he had embraced and loved and who had protected him in those days.

Later, Chin told her that not everyone could see beauty, so there was no need for her to be sad. She smiled. "I'm not sad at all," she said. Then tears flowed down her face.

The people of Cay Cong alley never saw the old man in the luxury car visit the Buoi Chieu House again.

There came a season when raindrops splattered on the roofs and Hong was no longer seen with her sweetened porridge. No longer did her sweet and sad voice ring out, nor did Chin drop in for a cup of tea at the Tu Bung Café.

She was seriously ill. He was devastated. Her talk would always turn to death until old Phi scolded her. "I'm much older than you, and I'm still here. So how can you talk of dying?"

The fifteenth of the Lunar March: as usual, a performance day at Buoi Chieu. Hong was still bedridden, but she insisted that she would sing. Chin applied her makeup and helped her to her chair. She sang the ancient songs: the lament for the fate of Queen Mother Duong Van Nga, torn between her debt to her country and her love for her family; the eternal wait of Quyn Nga, at her hand loom by the bridge, for the return of her warrior husband; the hard and faithful life of Chau Long, who silently served her husband's friend Luu Binh for three years until he won his Confucian laureate title; and the fate of To Thi, who turned to stone as she stood with her small son in her arms, awaiting the return of her disgraced husband. She sang and sang until she fainted.

By the time Chin got her into bed, she was already in a coma. The residents of Buoi Chieu all sang a last song to honor a genuine artist. In those final moments, she saw all of her relatives, and she saw her son also, and he finally called her "Mother." Her parents were there as well, and they pardoned her, and then she found herself in her native village and was happy in that place of her beautiful childhood.

Trang flowers fell from the trees in the yard.

Once, I dropped in at the Tu Bung Café and met old Chin Vu. He told me that he had spent his life following the drama troupe and that, in the end, it was worth it because he had finally been given a major role to play. What role was that? one of the other patrons asked. The son of actress Hong, he said. When the woman he had loved all her life was on her deathbed, he had been able to come to her and call her "Mother," and see her smile. Only that? Yes, only that, but how could you young people ever understand?

Translation by Nam Son and Wayne Karlin

XU HUIZHI

Four Poems

JULY THIRTY-FIRST

A usual day
A humpback whale crosses the meridian
Flying fish in files on the sea
Leap up, from yesterday to today

In dreams angels guard the hourglass
Counting the time God gave us
An afternoon nap lasts a millennium
A gaze, will be an eternity

I know
This is one of those usual days
Sitting on the whale's back
We cross the meridian

(2001)

SORROW

Sorrow makes one age

When I grow old I pray that you
You will still be beside me

Under the scorching sun
Our saliva and our hairs
Will evaporate and burn, instantaneously

DRUMBEAT

Parched thunderclaps in the wilderness
I can hear
Your drumbeat from far away

Purple hares softly weep
Stars lose their way on the snowy prairie

TO THE END OF THE SKY

Like a gale
A panther gallops across the prairie
And collapses suddenly
Wide-eyed gazelles die of thirst
An entire herd fallen by the waterhole
This is the summer of despair
A horror even greater than despair
Is spreading

A group of elephants in search of a gravesite
With no regard for distance
A blue hook of a moon
Hangs darkly at the edge of the sky
A conflagration will burn away all
O a conflagration will
Burn, from the seashore to the end of the sky

(2001)

Translations by Michelle Yeh

Three Poems

A HYMN TO HUALIAN

Blessed is the Lord for bestowing on us these gifts we are so unworthy
    of receiving.
The mountains of Hualian. The azure of a summer evening at the
    stroke of seven.
Deep sleep. The broad sweep of the sea tilting out of kilter on
    those hairpin
turns we take at sixty miles per hour. Love
and transgression. His injustices.
Your loveliness.

THE LAST SUPPER

I clench my fists to prevent
The wounds from breaking out in advance of the event

No one has the heart to speak up as you clasp your cigarette
Your fingers already forming the sign of the cross

But O there is a shaft of moonlight in my heart
Gleaming on the garden where you will rise from the dead

Each savory dish the skeptic sets before us is more delicious than
    the last
The love songs of the infidels outside the walls reduce me to tears

If there be a Judas among us
It must be that side of the fish not cooked to perfection

With more than our fill we grow drowsy and tired
And with that quite forget the sorrow

LES FEUILLES MORTES

The dead leaves
scrape across yesterday's lanais.

The violincello squeegees the car window
all through the night.

The numbers fallen from our calculations
crawl out through the crack under the door.

The rooms bellow in unison
to the now distant rain.

Translations by Steve Bradbury

Three Poems

WALKING

once we moved in an age of ideas and signs
debate's lexicon gouging at truth

we then entered a world of instruments and logic
trudging through wastes beyond hypotheses and equations

before soaring into a universe of introspection and dream
unfocussed consciousness like the 3000 layers of an onion of
worlds-within-worlds

these days, we walk in an age of replication and chatter
this limited life forging away specially for the sake of futility

new dilemmas hatch from outdated language
as fertile as ant nests

"love is universal but we are universally unable to love"
light goes in straight lines but it also curves

time is delusion, space illusion
no birth no death no filth no purity no increase no decline

must we go on walking whereverwards or will
wherever come walking towards us next?

NOTHINGNESS

waking from a world of nothingness
it could be that I don't even know
that I'm already dead

squirming maggots inside my body twist to form a double-helix
endowing it with the will of atoms
and consuming the memory of a lifetime

and so I commence the next phase of evolution
just as I once walked amongst the vast ranks of the living
I now   walk with the

indescribable
and yet apparently familiar ranks of the dead
to continue a journey that goes beyond knowledge

indeed
you cannot treat me with the knowledge of living alone
because you know nothing at all   about nothingness

indeed, nothingness is lighter than shadow
harder than concepts   stranger than light
simpler than death   or life

but there in the ranks I sense your shining non-existence
regret at your absence becomes a baffling summons
which finally allows me to brush past

nothingness   and amidst all the upset
to incarnate once more the infant of desire…

(1997)

I

me, I borrowed his body
and that segment of the flow of time

my coming into this world was like a surrealist painting
and from that moment—awesome—there was grief/joy

desire, and ambition—these I understand
although I'm only borrowing

but suddenly   I clean forgot   the full story
including the fact that I too was originally once a universe

and because of this, I have
elaborated games

with that being and the whole of this egg-shaped life
turning day and night into one another's dreamworlds

when I wake in another dream
I find that I've

unwittingly inscribed a poem
entitled   "I"

(1997)

Translations by Simon Patton

Three Poems

ON ENCOUNTERING SORROW

Translator's Note
> The speaker in this poem was Qu Yuan (343–278 B.C.E.), the first identifiable poet in China. A nobleman of the kingdom of Chu in the lake country south of the Yangzi River, Qu was slandered by fellow courtiers and banished to the southern hinterlands by the inconstant king, whom he calls the Fair One in this poem. The king of Huai was the father of the Fair One. Qu later drowned himself in the River Milo.—M.Y.

The South, you know
Is the Land of Promise…
Loving priestesses believed in this deeply

Then China had not yet taken shape
The chariot of the Sun God only reached River Huai,
    at most the Yangzi
Until Zhuanxu—my ancestor
The blood of the sage thawed, and flowed south
Millennia later
His blood reached the city Cheng
Cheng was just a land of swamps then
Invisible deities and spirits
Were everywhere in the air

The land of Dream Clouds—yes, the entire region
Was filled with orchids!

A few centuries passed by
The mists had dispersed
The rainy season ended

Chu became the South to be proud of
Once it even vied for the rule of the Central Plains
We worshipped the aesthetics of black lined in gold
Virtues of heady fragrances
A religion of tender love
Graceful, reserved, fancy-prone…

A more widely told story
Speaks of the secret marriage vow, between humans and gods
And spirits of fishhawks, daylilies, and
Morning dew

In the Month of Yin, the Year of Yin
My birth deserves mention
Especially because it preordained all
And witnessed all
The hour when Shen Ti shone in the northeast
The last light snow of the first month
Had just cleansed the early-blooming selinea
My mother—
Like so many mothers of Chu—
A mysterious, high-born
But obscure goddess
Placed me amidst mushrooms and cassias
Rinsed my soul
With the melting snow gathered from orchid buds
Thus setting in motion my never-cooling blood
At the age of twenty
I had a name the whole South adored
Lingjun—"Divine Balance"
But how could I have foreseen
The misfortune of possessing a mind of clarity?

Low, flat lakeshores
Are not fit for farsighted men
The Kingdom of Chu, with the inevitable
Coarseness of the first mold
Repeatedly wounds a delicate soul
Driving me to my wits' end
When standards of judgment have yet to be established
How can things of supreme beauty come into being?

But like the angelica in my hand
I too face the end of beauty and sweetness
In the vicissitudes of time

I have discovered
Death is the only unchangeable truth
Besides, without the ability to discriminate
Goodness turns into my suffering in the end—

How can you give a phoenix a mere foot of land?
How can you give the North Star only one night?

How could I not know my impatience
And cold eyes, those cold cold eyes?
They used their eloquence to slander me
Laying nails and hooks around the palace
To catch me by the train of my robe
Turning me into a silkworm spinning deliriously
But I had no time to grope around in their meandering alleys
When a newly written poem
Lifted me up to the sky of stars
But an unparalleled concern
Pulled me back down to my care

Yes, clattering horse hooves on the borders
Have shaken the pillars in the ancestral temple
A metallic taste has interrupted
The stay of the fragrant castor plant
The mighty Kingdom of Qin
Has eclipsed the fading twilight in the western sky
Sorry lies fabricated in the land of Shu
Led to the downfall of the noble King Huai

Fair One, Fair One, where should I begin?
Always he is on my mind
Like a pearl in the oyster…

That man, in the seat of honor
Showed me an appreciation beyond my belief
As if keeping a promise from the previous life
To take me to the granary among the clouds
Telling me of an unrequited love at six and passion at forty
The stern upbringing of his royal father, and
A territorial ambition that knew no tempering

We were both young then
We were unsophisticated, uncarved
Like a music score yet to be written
An icy river in one moment
A molten rock in the next

Moving, like clouds of thunder and lightning
Demure, like the most tender spring

But he made himself forget all of that, as decidedly
As a jade pendant dropping to the floor, breaking
The nine acres of orchids that I had grown laboriously
Lay fallow—
I entered the counsel chamber
Where foul weeds grew rampant
I entered the inner court
Where ghostly shadows and flattering rhetoric lingered
At last, we came face to face with each other
He pointed to the South
Without a shred of hesitation, concern, or care in his eyes.

He astonished me
In that moment
He acted in a truly royal way
Except for the head-spinning blindness
The heart-wrenching ruthlessness
He acted in a truly royal way
Yet
We were once the best of friends, truly
We were once so very close…

And the South, you know
Is the Land of Promise
The second time I came to the Yangzi shore
My clothes covered with dust
The humid heat of the continental climate
Was killing the pepper on the banks
A dusty gust began to rise
By the bright water's edge, a horned dragon
Recoiled in bitter pain
Its five-colored scales robbed by the rainbow

When the night falls
Laughter comes drifting from the cooling shores
In the land of Chu you find many folks like these
They don't insist on fauna and flora
Nor on aesthetics
They live in abodes of woven grass down the river
Fish for a living
And love telling fables
I cannot bear to look at them
For I am of different blood

Besides, I have fallen short in both
Self-cultivation and cultivation of the world

Solitude consumes me day by day
As if to close the shop early
Unsold flowers are left in the scorching sun
But in the beginning, you know
I knew nothing about abandoning
My intention to reconcile; my hope died and was reborn
Over and over again
Now I have given up on learning other possibilities

Where did I go astray?
For a while I was deeply attracted by myself
When the whole world was drunk
I gazed at myself by the pool where the giant Peng bird fell—
A special destiny requires a special man to complete
Every human being is unique
The inward-searching eye has opened

Now, dressed in selinea and shady angelica
My hair tied with sedges and thistles
Holding a bouquet of autumn orchids
I sing in the wilderness to my heart's content
The villagers living by the lake
Whisper among themselves
A little girl runs up to me
I present her with a bouquet of melilotus rods
A little boy runs up to me
I present him with a bouquet of cart-halting flowers
I climb up the round hill with great effort
A gusty wind renews my mood
Finally I can use a child's eyes
To know what I once knew—
And love—
The tired and exhausted
Kingdom
O Kingdom
My tears cannot help but pour like rain

When
Did the deities and spirits quietly withdraw?
When
Did the clouds cease to rest
And the dragon cease to snore lightly as it turns in its sleep?

When
Did the priestess's song lose its warmth?
The priestess's song   its warmth lost
For they have ceased to believe

But I have not wavered in my belief
The South is the Land of Promise
Worthy of all of my love
All of my bitter suffering

I will inscribe these words
On the flowing river.

(1982)

BANDIT'S SONG

A swallow brings spring in its beak
Builds a nest in the decrepit mountain den
Flies down the eaves on a fresh morning
And turns into a maiden fetching water to wash herself
Her slender body, willful and spirited, holds
A perseverance fit for long voyages
When I come back from my raids
I always run into her
And feel ashamed of my delinquencies of the night before
Past noon, she arrives on a breeze
Pecks at my sleepiness
Under the bow and arrows hanging on the wall
Making me unable to sleep
As she whispers an unsolved secret repeatedly

I occupy this land and claim myself king
Under the combined pressure of eternity and a senseless life
I live apart from the world
With the persistence and indulgence of an artist
I raise fowls of language and beasts of imagery
I envy others' autumn harvests of wisdom and stupidity
As my imagination declines day by day
Like a landfilled lake
My terrain gets shallower and shallower
Now and again the flag that invites me
To surrender invades my dreams

I occupy this land and claim myself king
Dream of practicing anarchy in my writing
Guard myself carefully, and
Hope that the memory of the swallow
Will prolong a career of rebellion
I am so bent on.

(1988)

FAREWELL (ON LONELINESS)

So, with an easel on my back, I head off to Algiers as a mercenary.
For I met another lonely soul in the wasteland, who stripped me
    of my only possession, solitude,
So I broke away from her arms despondently
On a rainy day when the rain had stopped.
Like a cup cracked from being shaken, my heart can't take any kind
    of affection
Or my traveler's air will disintegrate like a fugitive wind.

I stay in my room, patiently, carefully reassemble the blocks of my
    image that she knocked down,
So full of sorrow—O—seeing double pupils in my eyes.
I talk to myself endlessly to comfort the beastly wound, till loneliness
    rushes in like a steamroller charging into the living room.
So, I pick up the easel, cast an uncertain gaze toward the distance, on
    a rainy day when the rain has stopped.
All I see when I open my hands is fatigue, cool and tame.

My departure is like a flower seed,
But what if it doesn't fall on rich soil?
How could I bear, how could I bear the fact that my departure did
    not leave you with some regrets or sorrow?

(1976)

Translations by Michelle Yeh

Frontier Perspectives: Three Interviews on Contemporary Poetry in Taiwan

During the past five decades, Taiwan has evolved dramatically, from a little-known island into a nation-state with twenty-three million people and one of the largest economies in the world. Some of the best modern Chinese poetry comes from Taiwan, and the evolution of modern Taiwanese poetry is the story of how the periphery has transformed itself into the frontier—an open, cosmopolitan zone where experimental leaps are possible and boundaries easily crossed to create a poetry "in the wild." Michelle Yeh and I interviewed three major poets—Yang Mu, Ya Xian, and Luo Fu—to provide varied perspectives on the context and state of poetry in Taiwan. Each poet offers different insights, and through their differing perspectives and thoughtful and cogent responses, readers will gain a better understanding of a complex situation. In each interview, Michelle Yeh presented the questions we drafted.—**A.S.**

■ Yang Mu

Wang Ching-hsien, who writes as Yang Mu, was born in Hualian on the east coast of Taiwan in 1940. After majoring in English at Christian Tung-hal University, he earned a master's degree from the University of Iowa and a doctorate from the University of California at Berkeley. He is a professor of comparative literature at the University of Washington in Seattle and has served as the dean of the College of Humanities and Social Sciences at National Dong Hwa University. He has published thirteen books of poetry, and his poems are available in English in *No Trace of the Gardener: Poems of Yang Mu,* translated by Lawrence R. Smith and Michelle Yeh (Yale University Press, 1998). The following interview was conducted by telephone with Yang Mu in Taipei, on 14 July 2002.—**A.S.**

MY I'd like to start with a few thoughts and questions that relate to a general overview. The history of Taiwan is complex: exploited first by the Portuguese in the sixteenth century, then colonized by the Dutch and Spanish, annexed as a province of China during the Ch'ing dynasty, ceded to Japan in 1895 after the Sino-Japanese War, and retroceded to China at the end of World War II. I wonder how this history has made modern poetry in Taiwan unique and complex?

YM The poetry of Taiwan is bound to be different from poetry in mainland China. Not only does Taiwan have the memory of European colonialization, but Japan, a country with a fine culture, has exerted an influence also. Though in earlier times Taiwanese poets were not as concerned with aboriginal culture, they had some contact with it and had a degree of understanding and appreciation. That has had an impact on Taiwan's poetry too. In contrast to post-1949 mainland China, where politics has dominated poetry for decades, Taiwan has developed a strong poetic tradition.

MY For many years, you have gone back and forth between Taiwan and the United States. You currently teach at the University of Washington and have just completed your term as dean of the College of Humanities and Social Sciences at National Dong Hwa University in Taiwan. In terms of your own work, is it possible to think of Taiwan and the United States as forming a poetic axis? What effect has this back-and-forth motion had on your poetry?

YM I don't see any direct relationship between where I live and how I express myself artistically. In general, geographical location has little impact on me, since for many years I have not written about that kind of external reality. Any response I have to external reality takes a long time to sediment, so to speak, before I can write about it. Of course, living in different countries gives you a different perspective, psychologically and intellectually, and I think it plays a positive role in my writing. When I do write about locations, they tend to be smaller countries, such as Chechnya and Afghanistan. They move me deeply. I guess Seattle is like a hideout for me, where I can focus on writing. I don't know if that's good or bad. Sometimes, disturbances from the outside are good.

MY You say small countries move you. Is it because you identify Taiwan with them?

YM Only when I wrote about Chechnya did I consciously identify it with Taiwan. In that particular case, I feel that though the history of the two places is quite different, there is the same underlying urge, which I understand well. As a younger man, I was always moved by more obscure places; I would imagine such places as Turkey, India, and Tibet.

MY In the evolution of your poetry, I know you have had at least two pen names: Yeh Shan and Yang Mu. Years ago when Arthur was an undergraduate at the University of California at Berkeley, he encountered your poetry in Cyril Birch's *Anthology of Chinese Literature*. Under the pen name Yeh Shan—which can be translated as "fine jade leaves"—you wrote with a sensuous lyrical impulse. In 1972, you changed your pen name to Yang Mu. Can you tell us why?

YM The poems in Birch's anthology were written by a young man. It was hard for me to effect radical changes under the same name, although I treasure my early style.

MY You are well known as a scholar of classical Chinese poetry. How significant is classical Chinese poetry in your creative work? How do you draw on the classical tradition without being dominated thematically—formally or otherwise—by it?

YM Classical Chinese poetry has helped shape my poetry over the years. More and more I feel that what you read shapes your perspective and sensibility. In the past when I got involved in a literary debate and I did not want it to drag on, I would say, *There's no point in continuing this debate because we have read very different books. Our reading lists are different*—as simple as that. Long ago, even before I left Taiwan to study in the United States, I had resolved to read as much as I could. I have found that the things I read when I was young—whether it was classical Chinese or European literature—have had an enormous impact on my writing. I especially love classical European literature from before the Renaissance. A central image in my most recent book of poetry, *Ventures,* is the medieval knight.

As for classical Chinese poetry, I find it extremely useful in teaching me how to achieve musicality and manipulate tone of voice within a limited number of syllables. In the nearly century-long history of modern Chinese poetry, I have yet to find a poet who has achieved optimum musicality. But I find plenty of that in classical poetry, particularly *shi*. Unlike most Chinese readers, I am not that interested in song lyrics [*ci*] from the Southern Song on. Lately I've been reading Xie Tiao [A.D. 464–499]—Li Po's favorite poet—and love what he does with sound. In general, Chinese poetry before the T'ang dynasty is particularly inspiring for modern poets. Because the prosody for the quatrain and the regulated verse [dominant forms of classical poetry since the seventh century] had yet to be codified, those ancient poets relied solely on their own genius and a good ear to harmonize sounds and create musical patterns. Unlike later times, there was no prescription to follow, and every poem could sound refreshingly different—just like baseball, with each game being played differently. That's the fun of writing poetry.

MY It's interesting that you should say this. Many Chinese readers criticize modern poetry for its apparent lack of musicality. But based on what you've said, modern poetry is an even bigger challenge for the poet, since the length of the line varies far more than in ancient poetry.

YM Yes, in general there is the problem of musicality with modern poetry.

MY You once wrote in the afterword to *Someone* [1986], "If poetry, or the organic life of culture as a whole, is to be worthy of persistence, we must seek its definition in the process of experimentation and breakthrough." Should we think of this statement as a commitment to formal experimentation? Or is that too narrow an interpretation?

YM The statement is not just about formal experimentation but about expressing the essence of poetry. Though important, formal experimentation is a byproduct of experimentation with the question "What is poetry?"

MY What are you currently working on?

YM I am still writing about my childhood. Last July or August, I was in Seattle and was suddenly struck by a memory of a Jewish friend of mine whom I haven't seen for more than thirty years. His name is Matthew, but in the poem I change it to Isaac. I remember that when I was a graduate student at Berkeley, we saw each other a lot. When I was teaching at the University of Massachusetts at Amherst, one day he suddenly showed up and invited me to his home in Boston. He said he was going to Yugoslavia on an important mission. After some time, I saw him again and I asked him if he had carried out his mission. He replied, "I don't want to talk about it." I still don't know if he actually went to Yugoslavia. In fact, I think he might even be delusional. But I cherish this memory of Matthew, cherish his "craziness." More and more, I believe that literature deals with the abstract, which is universal.

MY The mainstream theory today is critical of any mention of universals; instead it emphasizes cultural differences. How would you respond to that?

YM Of course, literature from different cultures has different features or different modes of expression. I don't mean that all literature should be the same or that there are universal formulae. When I first went to the U.S., I didn't like Allen Ginsberg or William Carlos Williams. But after a while, I understood that *is* American poetry and respected that.

Many years ago, I attended a two-day conference on East-West comparative literature at Harvard University. I think it was 1971 or 1972. Near the end of the conference, a professor of English literature from UCLA raised a question: why is Chinese poetry so short? There were many established scholars of Chinese poetry present, but they asked me, a junior professor, to answer the question, so I said I'd try. I turned to the English professor and said, "Before I answer your question, I'd like to ask you a question: why is European poetry so long?"

I also believe that literature requires no historical or sociological background to be great. Bai Juyi [Po Chü-i] is a good example. Bai considered his New Music Bureau poems his most important work because of their profound social significance. And he dismissed the more personal poems as "leisurely writing." A thousand years later, however, the reverse is true. It is Bai's leisurely poems that are the most enduring.

MY So by "universal," you don't mean themes common to people regardless of cultural or historical background?

YM More than that. I'm also referring to technique, or mode of representation. Abstract poetry is like abstract painting or music. That kind of abstractness is universal.

■ **Ya Xian**

Ya Xian (Mute Strings) is the pen name of Wang Qinglin, who was born in Nanyang, He'nan Province, in 1932. In 1949, he joined the military and moved to Taiwan. In the 1960s, he was invited to the International Writing Program at the University of Iowa, and later he earned a master's degree from the University of Wisconsin at Madison. He was the chief editor of the *Epoch Poetry Quarterly, Young Lion Literature and Art,* and, for many years, the literary supplement of the *United Daily.* The poems he wrote in the 1950s and 1960s continue to exert a strong influence on poets in Taiwan. This interview was conducted by telephone with Ya Xian in Vancouver, on 4 July 2002, and was translated by Michelle Yeh.—**A.S.**

MY "From the beginning, modern Chinese poetry looked to foreign— predominantly Western—poetry for inspiration and alternative modes of writing." To what extent would you say this statement of mine is true today?

YX In the past, China and the West were seen as sharply polarized sources of inspiration. Poets used to be labeled either filial son or rebel. They had to choose to be one or the other. By now, I think, the dichotomy has been resolved. Younger generations tend to have a more international outlook. They blend Chinese and non-Chinese elements much more freely and unconsciously.

MY How would you describe the current situation of poetry in Taiwan?

YX Young poets today are freer in style and language.

MY This raises another question. How much imitation goes on between generations? Over the years we have seen many imitators of such major poets as Yang Mu, Luo Fu, and yourself.

YX Imitation does exist, but more in the past than now. I think young poets today are bolder and freer.

MY Poetry and literary journals and literary supplements to newspapers used to play a major role in the development of poetry in Taiwan. Is that still true today?

YX There are fewer poetry and literary journals today. *Epoch* and *Blue Star* are among the oldest. Literary journals such as *Unitas* and *Chung-wai Literary Monthly* also publish poetry regularly.

MY How do you feel about the general decline in poetry journals?

YX I'm not too worried about it. A new venue for poetry is the Internet. Internet literature is flourishing in Taiwan. Also, even though the old *Modern Poetry Quarterly* folded a few years ago, some of the editors got together and launched a new journal called *Now Poetry* [Xianzai shi]. The first issue has just come out.

   After I received it, I wrote to the chief editor, Hung Hung, and said that the new journal was earthshaking! It's an excellent issue.

MY One characteristic of the new issue is the considerable space devoted to song lyrics.

YX Yes. This is an interesting feature. In the 1950s to 1960s, we used to look down on song lyrics. When we dismissed a poem, we would say, "This is just song lyrics!" The attitude was partly due to the influence of Ji Xian [the veteran poet who founded *Modern Poetry Quarterly*], who made a clear distinction between poetry and songs. But since the Campus Folk Song Movement of the early 1970s, poetry has developed a close affinity with songs. Many modern poems have since been set to music—for instance, poems of Zheng Chouyu and Yu Kwang-chung. Even a few of mine. They are turned into new folk songs, popular songs, or art songs. Of course, you know that Hsia Yü is a professional song lyricist.

MY Do you have much contact with poets on the mainland?

YX   Not much. I have visited the mainland many times, but most of the time I only visit my hometown to pay respects to my deceased parents. But I have given a few lectures—at Peking University, for example—and attended a few poetry conferences on the mainland.

MY   In your view, are there significant differences between poetry being written in Taiwan and that on the mainland?

YX   There is a long, robust tradition of poetry as art in Taiwan. On the mainland, I think it's only in recent years that poetry has shed its ideological shackles and developed in the direction of art. Much of the literature in the 1980s was Scar Literature; even Misty Poetry was still an expression of social protest.

MY   Do you see much understanding or appreciation between poets on the two sides of the Taiwan Strait?

YX   I think the period of significant influence across the strait has passed. In fiction, mainland fiction was quite influential in Taiwan in the late 1980s and early 1990s. In poetry, Taiwanese poetry influenced mainland poets in the mid-1980s, including Misty poets like Menglongshi.

MY   Quite a few of the younger generation have switched from poetry to fiction. What's your view on that?

YX   It's true that it happens sometimes. But I believe that poetry has played a significant role in molding contemporary fiction, both in terms of narrative language and the extensive use of imagery. Sometimes I find the fiction by former poets more like prose poetry than fiction. The boundary between prose and poetry seems to be blurred.

■ **Luo Fu**

Luo Fu (also written Lo Fu) is the pen name of Mo Luofu, who was born in Hengyang, Hunan Province, in 1928. He joined the military during the Sino-Japanese War (1937 to 1945) and moved to Taiwan in 1949. He graduated with a degree in English from Tamkang University and has been a full-time writer and translator since. While stationed in southern Taiwan in 1954, he founded the Epoch Poetry Society with Zhang Mo and Ya Xian, serving as the editor of the *Epoch Poetry Quarterly* for more than a decade. In the 1960s and 1970s, he was a controversial figure, involved in many literary debates. A book of his available in English is *Death of a Stone Cell,* translated by John Balcom (Taoran Press, 1993). The following interview was conducted by mail with Luo Fu in Vancouver, on 9 July 2002, and was translated by Michelle Yeh.—**A.S.**

MY Have poets in Taiwan drawn equally from the Chinese and the Japanese traditions?

LF The three sources of influence on the poets of Taiwan are traditional Chinese, modern Western, and modern Japanese literatures. At the risk of being politically incorrect, allow me to differentiate two groups of Taiwanese poets: those from mainland China around 1949, and the local Taiwanese.

First, the locals. Taiwan was colonized by Japan for half a century. Many poets received a Japanese education, and for them Japanese literature was a major influence. Some of them did not learn how to write in Chinese till after 1945 and are known as the translingual generation, including such poets as Lin Hengtai, Huan Fu, and Chen Xiuxi. However, the middle-aged and younger generations are not as close to Japanese poetry as their predecessors but rather are more interested in representing native society and culture. Some of them have leanings toward political writing, and some pursue poetry written in Fukienese.

Those who emigrated to Taiwan from the mainland around 1949 were influenced by traditional Chinese literature, May Fourth literature [of early-twentieth-century China], and Western modernism. Although Western modernism was dominant in the early days, a call for a return to tradition emerged in the 1970s, and many poets consciously shifted from "horizontal transplantation" to "vertical inheritance." They began to reevaluate traditional Chinese culture and explore classical Chinese poetics. Perhaps I can say that postwar poetry was most original, but modern poetry reached its maturity in the 1980s, when Western modernism and traditional Chinese aesthetics converged after decades of experimentation.

MY How has surrealism been a significant influence on your own work and on modern poetry in Taiwan in general?

LF In the 1950s to 1960s, poets were highly receptive to Western modernism. Western influence mainly came from two directions: existentialism and surrealism. Surrealism flourished in Europe between the world wars, and by the 1950s it had declined. However, it was extremely attractive to Taiwan's poets for two reasons. First, those who fled to Taiwan with the Nationalist government found themselves disoriented and dispossessed. Further, they lived in a repressive society where there was limited freedom of speech. The nightmarish history and political reality exerted enormous pressure on the poets, who desperately needed an outlet for their frustration. The mode of expression and imagistic language of surrealism fulfilled that need without getting them into trouble with the regime.

Secondly, at that time the language and techniques of modern poetry were still overshadowed by May Fourth vernacular poetry, which tended to be plain and straightforward. It could not adequately express the interior world, nor could it represent modern life with its distinct pace and rhythm. Therefore, many poets turned to Western modernism for new modes of expression. They started out with French symbolism and gradually embraced surrealism. They also tried to integrate surrealism with traditional Chinese poetics—to Sinicize it, so to speak—thereby creating a new language, a new sensibility, a new poetics.

Exposure to surrealism began with translations of French poetry, so its influence grew slowly and organically. Ya Xian's "Abyss" and my *Death of a Stone Cell* were among the first surrealist works in postwar Taiwan. In 1964, I also translated "The Origin of Surrealism" and wrote a series of essays titled, respectively, "Surrealism and the Purity of Poetry," "Surrealism and Modern Chinese Poetry," and "Surrealist Poetry and Zen." Other poets influenced by surrealism include Shang Qin, Guan Guan, Xin Yu, Bi Guo, Luo Ying, and Su Shaolian. Nowadays, I don't see any surrealist in the younger generation.

MY   What poets in the West do you admire, and for what reasons?

LF   Among French poets, my favorites are the early modernists, such as Baudelaire, Rimbaud, Valéry, and Apollinaire. As for Anglo-American poets, I like Wallace Stevens more than T. S. Eliot. Eliot is too intellectual, even a little pedantic at times. Stevens's poetics is closer to my own. In the early days, I was also fascinated by Rilke. I learned how to effect a dialogue with God through my poetry. I found Rilke highly religious, with a profound, pure consciousness of life. There are traces of Rilke in my early work *Death in a Stone Cell* and in my new poem sequence, *Driftwood*.

MY   You have had much contact with poets in mainland China. In your view, how are Taiwan and the mainland similar or different?

LF   Some people may think that since poets on the two sides of the Taiwan Strait use the same language—Chinese—their poetry must be similar. This is wrong. Poets in Taiwan draw from written Chinese; it is more traditional, more indebted to classical literature. Poets on the mainland grew up on Russian literature and Maospeak. For a long time, poetry was a political instrument. The emergence of Misty Poetry in 1980 may be seen as a literary revolution with profound ramifications, and the Misty poets are the first generation of modernism on the mainland. Misty Poetry was heavily influenced by translations of foreign literature and had little to do with the Chinese tradition. It is not until the third and fourth generations that poets have begun to develop their own language and styles.

MY   You immigrated to Vancouver in 1996. What was the reason for the move? What change in your art has developed as a result? What are you working on?

LF   Since I moved to Vancouver, I rarely go out. My social circle consists mainly of Chinese writers in the area. So, in a way, immigration is no different from moving into a new study. I call my immigration "the second exile." The first exile was in 1949, when for political reasons I moved to Taiwan. The second exile has nothing to do with politics and is based on my own choice. I chose Canada because I wanted to find a safe, peaceful place as the final stop on the journey of my life. Also, I hoped that the new environment would take my writing to a higher level.

Living in a foreign land, I feel like the great Peng bird from Zhuangzi's "Free and Easy Wandering." I enjoy the freedom, but sometimes I feel lonely too. To while away time, I read, write calligraphy, and garden. The pastoral life of a hermit has also inspired me to write poetry. In winter, I often sit before the window and write. I have written a few poems about snow, and I call my study Snow Pavilion. In October 1997, I traveled to Alaska with my old friend Wai-lim Yip; I was deeply moved by the grandeur of nature. After I came back, I wrote a poem just under two hundred lines titled "The Great Glacier." My calligraphy has been exhibited in New York, Kuala Lumpur, mainland China, Taiwan, and Vancouver. In January 2000, I put aside all distractions and started working on a long poem sequence. It was completed in one year, and totaled three thousand lines. The title is *Driftwood*. On New Year's Day 2001, the poem appeared in the literary supplement to the *Liberty Times* in Taiwan and was serialized for three months straight. In August 2001, the book was published by Unitas. I consider *Driftwood* a landmark in my career. It sums up my experience of exile, my artistic explorations, and my metaphysics. I consider it a personal epic and the greatest achievement in my old age.

YANG MU

Fallen Leaves

Translator's Note

　　　　The 2-28 Incident refers to the riot of Taiwanese people in protest against the Nationalist government and its brutal suppression. The riot was triggered by an incident that took place in Taipei on 28 February 1947. The Incident was a taboo subject under the Nationalist regime until the lifting of martial law in 1987. Since then, the government has made an official apology to the victims' families and erected a memorial statue.—M.Y.

1

How does an awakened heart examine the blood trails of old
under the remnant icewalls of thorns, snakeberries, and
caltrops? Leaning, I listen to how the beetles and chrysalises
measure with their humble trails the obscure path
from death to rebirth, the journey we have vowed
to take, all the actions of a pilgrimage
and our questioning. When the scorching
sun first enters a shared night
and moderates the temperature, so that our earth
can obtain a solid intellectual basis as it turns at an angle
how the moon in its own track of revolution, in total eclipse
intimates the law of human partings and togetherness. But we
still argue the night before our journey
about each other's direction, deepening in the impassioned
　　darkness of last night
—the disintegration of desire, watermarks on frosted glass
drawing repeatedly dragon-patterns, a sketch of ethical
symbols—the memory of spring rain tapping the window
a relentless debate. But before the day breaks
the rain has stopped, the group of pilgrims
left a long time ago. Partridges coo far and near

2

Summertime, we live in the village of orange orchards, evenings
we listen to Granny's stories about the old war and close family
up till the time of the 2-28 Incident. In the mixed scent of
    mosquito repellant
and jasmines wafting from the yard I fall asleep
Dreaming of carefree flying, like a red-crowned crane thrusting forth
from the matting of a Chinese scroll, an almost transparent
    snow-white
spreading its large cartwheel wings, floating amidst
an ascending range of mountains. Time shifts its balance
in the wind, changing speed as it pleases
The seven colors of the cosmos turn instantaneously
casting me behind in the dim, ever-widening net
at the nexus of dots and lines, broken connections and curves
I bid a silent farewell to yesterdays
The scattered clouds and layered greenness, at this moment
under my gaze at a counterclockwise reality
take on a coloring from the foothills and the peaks—
melting into sea-blue angelic eyes, looking down
at the lush vegetation world in the great heat
Locking in the seasonal pattern of decay, pointing to a rebirth
like written words illuminating

3

Revolving like this toward a key entity
the final completion. The dew drips white drops first
on the dense slender-eyed foliage of aging trees
A falling star glides off the southwest sky unexpectedly
near the water, soon after the midnight frost
Frost flies up the unpainted wattle fence, we
look up from our books. Perhaps it's the last
fireflies of the year hurrying from the scattered classics
to prove that reading could also mean the collapse of
private imaginings; or it's the virus of creativity spreading
to the dark night as sweet as fruit juice. Crickets
screech in the drafty western chamber where we comprehend
decay as we sit down to read *Songs of the South*
till all the stars have changed their seasonal colors
indicating work done, and our stagnant thoughts
can't keep up with the universe revolving in greatness
outside the window, toward an organic completion

I sit up to inquire, pressured like never before
Nebulous clouds surge and sail on
A leaf falls, making the windchime sing

4

Then your magic mirror begins to reveal to us
all the expediencies. Sure enough:
Earth always slants toward the domain of dreams
when the heart is at its bleakest
Without hesitation, I choose the day
when the sea shows the first signs of cooling
In the woods small creatures like sparks of memory
their hair growing fast on the back, scamper
in the clearings covered with dry twigs and leaves
The owls of reason hoot, bouncing echoes
shake some trees from time to time
even impact the dimmest sunset
after the first snowfall, when you sit facing north
in front of the window punching on the computer keyboard
while I, under the lamp, reread the early Virginia Woolf
I can hear a tree, perhaps more than one
roaring like a rolling tide, leaning toward the dark
land. The snow becomes heavier all of a sudden
a white crane flies up in fright, perches on
another branch, its wings closing, an image of purity from
    one to zero

(2001)

Translation by Michelle Yeh

from The Salmon's Encounter with Death

3

The moment an eagle swoops down
Out of the sky above a river valley and
Seizes
A diaphanous layer of moonlight from the water's surface
Time is silenced
As our tale unfolds

Once we swim upstream from the sea
The Adam's River becomes eloquently mute
The grassy banks dreary
The fog harder to control than ever imagined
So pale the morning
Changing by afternoon, speech slurred
The turbulent waters are gone
The river gradually grows colder
Leaves fall
Autumn floats and sinks
The water's words
Sputter on dangerous shoals
The fallen leaves are silent as autumn sheds tears
There's absolutely no need for such classical cruelty
The road extends to the horizon
Precipices and plains are all part of the course
In the great wave of Change
There is no need for joy or sorrow
And even less need to stubbornly insist that
I'm that bubble amid Change
Fear is unnecessary
Anger is unnecessary
Excessive concern is unnecessary
Living, or dying, for a philosophy
Also

Unnecessary
God exists in the breaths we take
And in the
Breathing of a
Blood-engorged louse
Reverence is unnecessary
Excessive faith is like extra fat
Piety is unnecessary
Before constructing the garden of life
We were choked
With all sorts of poisonous weeds
And God
Was speechless
Our only enemy is time
Before the dream is done
The course of life is run
A plume of smoke
Rises into the empty sky
Silently disperses
Vanishing into a greater nirvana
To deny illness   unnecessary
To prevent fading and aging   unnecessary
To cling, it is said, is more toxic
And, of course, unnecessary
To renounce   unnecessary
To be renounced   also unnecessary
Open-mindedness   unnecessary
Transcendence   unnecessary
Demons   good and bad, all unnecessary
The Buddha   plucking a flower and smiling also unnecessary
A short life
Spent looking for the key
Entirely unnecessary
The door   let it hang open
The clouds   let them float by

At this, time mumbles
Something that can't be heard
Words
Expressed from deep within
    Spoken for the water and mud
    Spoken for the insects in the grass
    Spoken for the flying birds and the stars
But our words
Are caught deep in our throats, frozen

A torch
Bound with rusted wire
Its aim not to burn
But to
Burn out and
Turn to ashes in a cold, cold ending
As we float and sink
Controlled and oppressed by language
There is nothing we wish to say
On the verge of death
We face an unknown face
In a blank space
We read a greater blank
First our form and color change
The minute changes of Change
Setting us apart, actually it's
A hook-shaped lower jaw
That grows out of our
Bodies (the invasion of an alien prior to death?)
Our spines
Ever so slightly
Begin to bow (perhaps concealing the unsolvable mystery of life)
And overnight our bodies turn red
What does this foretell?
Red has always been a serious illness
The river flushes
The reeds flush   the pebbles
Flush, the lichens flush
The marine animals flush
The peeping moon hiding on the peak flushes
The breathing of the Adam's River is red
Our Lord
Pauses wearily atop the clouds
His face red
Red at times is also the dispersed text of a foul speech
And is even a knife
For carving holes in human flesh and
Burying gunpowder
But we believe in something cooler
The church keeps a god
A nest of rats
As well as solitude
A bloodless solitude
Deeper than a wound
A wound deeper than a frown

A frown
Deeper than a prayer in a dark room

What tidings from the universe
Transcend worldly experience?
Life, at best,
Is just a heap of copper and iron scrap
That once clanged and rang
Beneath the rust the persistence remains
The dignity is still there
A heavy blow will still raise sparks
And at dignity's side is
Desolation
A little further on
Helplessness
Scaled
A demon is uncovered
Scaled again
The demon burrows deeper within
Our greatest effort in life
Is just to meet
A god
Not necessarily the One in Heaven
We continue to swim upstream
The shoals are covered with broken stones
Our wounds silent
We cannot hear our own hoarse cry
Fate
Is another magical gene
That does not allow us to stop
Fins tattered
Skull cracked
Bellies upturned float heavenward first
Prayer is a pair of superfluous hands
That reach out
To be grasped by no one
The Great Compassion Mantra
Is more vicious and gnawing than hunger
All that's left of us is a wound
A kind of incurable despondency
Our final days are
Perhaps the start of yet another storm
Our commerce is with fate
Neither buying nor losing
On the chopping block we are accustomed

To displaying a meekness borne of fatalism
The significance of the flesh
Is understood only by hungry wild bears and
Ravenous maggots
But the soul
Utters a piercing scream
As it slides along a porcelain platter
Into the choking stench of time's tunnel
In life there are two solemn and sacred things
Making love
And death
The only thing separating them is a thin, cool mist
Moreover   with no love
Vows to the contrary are as silly as a lump of flesh on the forehead
Laying eggs: the genesis of chaos
Depositing milt: the beginning of creation
Gracefully and gently
We embrace a universe
At that moment, a key falls from the sky
Is gently inserted
Into a dark room, moist and deep
A cold and ponderous body
Disturbed, a beast struggles inside
The chemical reaction of lust
Emits a cool fragrance of snow
Finally, a chorus of guardian angels in Heaven raise their voices
     in song
All doors hang open
All windows are flung wide
Heavenly light shines straight down
Far away
Death knells and bells of rebirth ring in unison

This has nothing to do with church
This has nothing to do with the ebb and flow of waters
This has nothing to do with a solitary eagle
Perched on a cliff. Grass withers
But perhaps sprouts again after a night of rain
This rabbit logic is laughably simple
Actually, it has nothing to do with rabbits or being laughable
It has nothing to do with lust
For cold are the sparks raised by love
You just have to believe it
Only DNA
Is a perfect egg

It can only be
Incubated slowly, not rushed
This is the only principle
Of mating, or masturbation

Translation by John Balcom

Ka-Shue (Letters Home)

Playwright's Note

I am Eurasian by ethnicity, a fourth-generation New Zealander. Based on the Chinese side of my family (the Tung clan of Bak-Chuen), *Ka-Shue* uncovers some of the last 150 years of a buried history in New Zealand. There has been a noticeable absence of a Chinese voice in this country. Perhaps it is because the Chinese community has been producing its own work for its own people, but this work has been largely inaccessible to a wider public until now. The material has often been spoken in Chinese, and not produced for mainstream audiences.

In writing *Ka-Shue* I have focused on the personal and domestic lives of three generations of a Chinese family. *Ka-Shue* spans the cultures of New Zealand and China, encompassing a broad sweep of the political events between the two countries as a backdrop for the personal dramas of the characters. This play is dedicated to my family.

I am aware that this play is close to the bone as far as my family history is concerned, but I hope in the end that I have attempted a universal story about immigration, about the systematic alienation of particular immigrant groups. For me *Ka-Shue* is also a story about immigrant women, struggling to make for themselves a sense of home and identity.

The play works most effectively with minimal props and furniture, which remain on stage throughout. Descriptions such as the venetian blinds of the hotel windows or Paw paw's graveside can be lit areas played out to the audience. *Ka-Shue* is set in several time frames—1939, 1941, 1945, 1959, and 1989—and the scenes weave seamlessly between them. *Ka-Shue* can be played by one actor or a full cast (as a series of monologues). If one actor is used, it is preferable to use only one costume and have the actor portray character changes through voice and body.

Time and place can be evoked with the help of live music (preferably with a blend of Western and traditional Chinese instruments). The ghost's movements are loosely based on the performance style of the Peking Opera and should be graceful and surreal, as if she is the link between the living and the dead.

My parents, Mayme Chanwai and
Michael Earle, New Zealand, circa 1962

Cast of Characters

Played by one actor:

JACKIE LEUNG-TAYLOR
Abbie's daughter. Born in New Zealand. Fourth-generation
New Zealander. Eurasian. Student in her early twenties.

ABBIE LEUNG
The mother. Born in China. Divorcée. Cantonese.
New Zealand Chinese business woman.

PAW PAW
The grandmother. Born in China. 'Old' Chinese. Conservative.
Hard working. Owns and runs the family green grocer shop
in Wellington. Gung gung's 'First Wife.'

GUNG GUNG
The grandfather. Born in China. 'Old' Chinese. Conservative.
Always well dressed. Addicted mah-jong gambler.
Has three wives and a concubine, Lady Li.

THE GHOST, LADY LI
Gung gung's concubine. Birth mother to Abbie. Committed
suicide shortly after Abbie was born.

Mentioned:

NIGEL TAYLOR
Jackie's father. Abbie's ex-husband. Pakeha
(referred to by Paw paw as the 'guilo'—foreign white devil).

CYRIL
Abbie's older half-brother. Their mother's favourite child.

GREAT AUNTY YING
Sister of Paw paw.

Act One

The stage is bare except for a wooden chair, a small camphor wood chest and a long, red backdrop centre upstage. The Ghost's headpiece is suspended just above head height in front of the red backdrop. To the left and right of the backdrop stand two waist-high plinths. A cigarette in a holder and a cigarette lighter sit on one plinth. A mock-up of a baby in swaddling sits hidden near the red backdrop. The following props sit on the chest: a 1940s telephone, rice bowl and chopsticks, brandy balloon with cognac, mah-jong piece, a knife, a single white rose, an ashtray, a dictaphone, and two pieces of folded red paper that act as mail. Several long red cloths (similar to the backdrop) and a white baby blanket lie in a heap at the base of the chest. A pen, writing pad, photograph, and handkerchief sit on the chair.

There are no costume changes or breaks. The actor remains on stage the whole time, dressed in a simple black Mandarin-style garment that can serve the character and gender changes. The garment has a pocket that conceals a large gold chain and locket. The Ghost is the only character who stays mainly centre upstage under the red backdrop. Throughout the performance a musician (off to the side) plays a range of traditional and modern instruments, evoking the time and place.

Scene One

Kwangtung Province, China, 1940.

The Ghost is standing centre upstage under the headpiece. She speaks in broken English with a Cantonese accent, accompanied by sounds of a wind chime.

GHOST My father name me. Shrimp Dumpling! He eating Har gow 蝦餃 when I born. Har gow 蝦餃! Shrimp Dumpling? [*laughs*] Maybe he want boy?! Later I name myself. Can't work in House of Heavenly Delight with name like that…Lady Li 驪夫人, that's what I call myself, after Concubine Li 驪姬. I love that name. My amah 阿媽 call me that, from old story. Say I look like her, when I little. She was famous for her scheming. When my daughter was born, I gave her my real name— Shrimp Dumpling. Her father call her Abbie…and then they left me…

She sees the baby taken. She falls to her knees, crying out desperately.

Abbie!…Abbie! Shrimp Dumpling!!…

At least something of me will live on… [*sardonic*] They say now 1989, Lunar Year of Snake 蛇年. Good year. April 5th. Legend of the Clear Bright Festival 清明節的傳説. Good time for celebrations. Also good time for suicide. Grave-sweeping time…

She re-enacts taking her own life, falling to the floor.

Lights and music change, the scene shifts to:

Scene Two

Saturday, June 3, 1989, a room in the Minzu Hotel not far from Tiananmen Square 天安門廣場, Beijing.

It is mid-afternoon, summer, and hot. Sunlight filters through half-shut venetian blinds. There are sounds of student protests from the street below. The sounds are menacing, and yet Jackie, who is looking out the window, is in an excited state, holding pen and paper. She can smell smoke. She stifles a cough and turns to the audience.

JACKIE You know, it's strange. The air's so thick here. I thought it was the smog, then I realised—the buses were burning! It was 3 P.M., I'd just started writing this letter to Mum when I smelt it. They'd pulled the seats out of the buses, turned them into toilets, porta-loos! [*laughs nervously*] And now they're on fire…Shit, burning shit!

Jackie is writing a letter to her mother, earlier that day. She addresses the audience.

Saturday, June 3rd, 1989. Minzu Hotel, Beijing. Hi Mum. How are you? I'm stuck in this mad city. Managed to bribe my way into this hotel. It's put a dent in the old credit card but it's great to be out of the heat. [*remembers*] Oh!—Give my love to Paw paw 婆婆—is she any better? I'm sure she won't be sick much longer, she's such an old dragon. What does she think about my sudden whim to go to China? Deep in the heart of Communist territory! Gung gung 公公 would probably turn in his grave. He hated the PRC. [*stops*] I know what you think, but I reckon he was a good person, at heart, even though you were always fighting. He was the best grand-dad. Gung gung 公公 and his mah-jong 麻將! [*pause*] Hey—how's Wellington? Must be cold now. It's stinking hot here at the moment. Mind you, it's worse in tent city. It's choked with students, hundreds of them. You must have heard about it? Tiananmen Square 天安門廣場—um, some of the students here are…protesting. [*rushing on*] Peaceful demonstrations. Nothing to worry about. It started when…what's-his-name died…Communist Party General something. Only one who'd listen, all they want is democracy! [*with a sense of wonder*] They've come from all over—Taiwan, Hong Kong. The Hong Kong students brought heaps of brand-new blue tents shaped like igloos and they set up in the Square. Tent city! The other night they built a huge white statue like the Statue of Liberty—called it the Goddess of Democracy. Placed it right in front of Mao's picture! We arrived—that is, Paul and I arrived a few days ago. Remember? [*smiling*] The Chinese student! The one I met in Hong Kong. He's been a fantastic friend. Well…more than that. Paul is here to write a report about the protest. [*defiantly*] You're not surprised that I have a Chinese boyfriend, are you? [*looking out the window*] China's amazing. It's wild. It's changed heaps since you were here. You know what you said about your permed hair and your make-up? How you stood out so much? The only Chinese woman in the whole of China with curly hair? It's not like that now. I've seen quite a few women in the latest trendy gear from Hong Kong. I'm sure it's all for the best. Hey! Some of the students defaced Mao's portrait and nothing happened. No recriminations! The government just stuck another in its place. They must have a huge warehouse filled with his images or something. Just like life here, really. Replaceable. [*recalls*] Hu Yaobang 胡耀邦…Hu Yaobang 胡耀邦! Former Communist!… [*laughs, smiles*] I've got a photo of me and Paul in Kwangchow, on our way to Beijing. By the Pearl River珠江. I thought you'd like this one Mum. It's at sunset, too. [*shows photo*] Paul looks great, doesn't he? It was such a romantic place. I wanted to stay…

She is startled back to the present, puts the photo down. She speaks to the audience.

Paul's changed. Hyper since we got here. Got it in his head he can make a difference. Working really hard. Too hard. Sleeping out in tent city. Thinks it's wonderful if you can't find a place to shit unless there's a queue a mile long. 'You're just soft, Jacqueline,' that's what he reckons. [*backing away from the window uneasily*] I want to be with him. But it's like a sea out there. So many people. I feel like I'm being swept away when I step onto the street…

Lights and music change, scene shifts to:

Scene Three

China, 1937, the interior courtyard of the Tung clan home, Kwangtungsang.
The music is evocative of old China. Paw paw 婆婆, as a young woman, is unfurling one long red cloth and refolding it in agitated sweeping motions as if it were household linen.

PAW PAW [*angry*] Listen to me, Ma! I want be with him. He need me. I look after him better than her. She no use for New Zealand, she not even educate! [*derisive*] Who she think she is? Lady Li 驪夫人! [*spits*] He got no use for concubine! I give him son already. Cyril, his son. I am first wife, Mrs Leung 梁太太 over there for New Zealand. Official. Allow only one wife. 1939, official! [*pause*] Ma, please, not be angry I leave

you. My place with my husband. We make lot of money錢, bring you
to New Zealand. I…I give, give my husband many healthy boy.
Plenty more grandson for you. We send money錢 back. You see. It
for best…

She lets the cloth drop slowly, close to tears.

Maybe father forgive me…

She turns away quickly. Lights and music change, scene shifts to:

Scene Four

China, 1940.
  The Ghost stands under the headpiece, centre upstage.

GHOST [*giggles, fanning herself*] You think I kill myself? I trick you…I dead
  already!

  *She lights up a cigarette on the end of an elegant holder and takes a
  long drag.*

  Many year ago, in springtime of our history, there was Concubine
  Li驪姬. Old Emperor dote on her. She want her own son be crown
  prince. So she kill Emperor son, then she begin reign of persecution
  to kill grandson of old Emperor, Chong Er重耳. Of course he run
  terrified, run away with his loyal men…wouldn't you? [*drags on cig-
  arette*] You surprise see me smoke? [*smiles, coy*] I know this trick—
  well, sort of trick, with cigarette. My lover taught me. [*laughs*] You
  always pull three out, from centre of packet, like this:

  She demonstrates using her fingers as the cigarettes.

  Pull middle one highest. If man take lowest one, it mean he afraid of
  you. If he take highest, it mean he has no respect. Be very careful.
  [*smiles*] Specially if he born in Year of Snake蛇年. If he take one not
  tall, not short, he make good business with you.

*She laughs, taking another long drag on her cigarette. Lights and music change,
scene shifts to:*

Scene Five

Wellington, New Zealand, June 1989.
  *Abbie's sitting room, evening. Abbie is smoking the cigarette from the previous
  scene. Located on the chest are the dictaphone and the white rose. Abbie is in the*

process of recording a letter to Jackie. She is busy around her sitting room. The music is light and cheerful underneath. Daydreaming, she suddenly remembers her dictation.

ABBIE Oh sorry, Jacqueline darling! Anyway, I hope you're eating properly. Things are much the same here…apart from these tourists. A Swedish couple have gone missing in the Coromandel. Just disappeared. It made me think of you in Asia. Remember you promised not to hitch? Who'd think it could happen in New Zealand?

Abbie pauses at the chest, regards the white rose for a moment, then places it downstage. Meanwhile she continues to speak in the direction of the dictaphone. She shifts the chair closer to the chest so that she can reach the ashtray, then seats herself comfortably. As she settles she picks up the dictaphone, speaks directly into the microphone, a little too loudly at first.

Oh, that's right. Another great-uncle has gone…went to the funeral, but I left early. Couldn't stand the gossip. Old Aunty Ying 瑛阿姨 and her cronies were very nice to my face but I swear I could read their thoughts: 'Ooh look, isn't that Abbie, what'sername? Ah. Married the guilo 鬼佬. Her mother quite sick, in hospital, poor thing…' [*defensive*] Poor thing! I went to see your Paw paw婆婆—she's not sick. [*laughs*] Probably outlive us all. Still grumpy as ever! Well—I took her some flowers, but she said they made her sneeze. Complained about the food at the hospital. So I cooked her winter melon soup. 'Not enough lotus nut' so I bought some dim sum from Wah's—even though she's not allowed it. 'Too salty!' Oh well. Hope you're looking after yourself.

She finishes her cigarette in silence, picks up the folded red paper—reading the 'mail' from Jackie.

Oh Jacqueline, you move around so much. I hope you've still got enough money錢—teaching English doesn't pay that well. Damn! Is this…Kwangtungsang廣東省? I can't read the return address, love. Who's this Paul? Not another 'lost puppy' I hope. Be careful. In China, I mean. I know it was a while ago that Nigel and I were there, but things don't always change. They whitewashed it all right—the Cultural Revolution. Have you been through Kwangchow廣州 yet? Make sure you do! When the sun's setting…I remember all these people, doing Tai-chi太極拳 on the banks of the Pearl River 珠江 …their slow unified movements against the brilliant golden sunset …[*pause*] One of the few times I've indulged in a truly romantic moment with your father. [*changes the subject*] 1974. The Revolution. It had an impact. [*laughs*] Our educational tour party were given performances by little Red Guards. And everywhere we went, there they were—groups of children doing skits lampooning Americans. [*laughs*] We were shown a medical centre in Wuhan and someone asked the doctors how China dealt with unwanted pregnancies. 'China has no such problem!' [*pause*] Slogans, character posters everywhere and I couldn't understand a word of it. There I was, Chinese in China and I didn't know my own language. [*pause*] Don't forget to visit the Wall and wrap up really warm. It can get cold enough to freeze the balls of a brass monkey as Nigel would say. Especially there…It was so empty. Like a great snake of crumbling brick that stretched beyond the horizon. [*laughs abruptly*] For God's sakes don't go ice-skating. Remember what happened to your father.

She places the dictaphone down on the chest, moving about her living room. Abbie is tidying up, placing the chair back and folding up the red cloth. Eventually she ends up next to the chest where the dictaphone is sitting.

And what's all this talk about Tiananmen? Only thing on telly here is the Swedish couple I mentioned. Absolutely shocking. [*chuckles at herself*] Listen to me go on…where was I? Oh yes, you'd better be careful about the water. Don't forget to boil it and for God's sakes don't join any protests—you can't save the world. I know I'm rabbiting on, dear, but you've got to be really careful over there. [*laughs*] The trouble with us Chinese is that we're supposed to be inscrutable…

Lights and music change:

Scene Six

The Hotel Selwyn, Wellington, 1949.

    Gung gung 公公, *impeccably dressed. It seems as if he is surrounded by cigar smoke. He regards the audience for a moment, then he picks up the mah-jong* 麻將 *piece and the brandy balloon containing a liberal dash of cognac. He speaks in broken English.*

GUNG GUNG Need four people for balance. Never play against pregnant woman—is bad luck. [*chuckles*] Washing tiles in middle first, make four walls, four wind. Chinese mah-jong 麻將 always play using your head. Very tricky. Keep in head what they throw away. Like this, you see.

He holds up the mah-jong 麻將 *tile.*

Bamboo tile 竹牌. Be flexible. But be careful! Always watch opponent eye. If blink more than three time, mean he nervous. That good sign.

Dealer start, throw dice, put more money 錢 down later. My little girl Abbie. She learn play also. Even if losing, go gracefully. Be as if losing thousand pound—nothing! Never let opponent see you upset. Abbie very good. I teach her myself. She ten now. [*laughs, shaking his head*] Too young to play with us. Chinese mah-jong 麻將 very lucky game, build wall of secrecy. Always race to win, but mustn't seem in big hurry. Suddenly in last hand, you come quietly to kill.

He sips the cognac, satisfied.

My little girl play piano too. Very good. Beethoven Moonlight… Sonata! Wear special red dress for Babaa 爸爸. Very pretty. Like her mother, Lady Li 驪夫人…[*coughs*] Stay up for guest, make them happy see little girl play pretty sound. I say 'play for Babaa 爸爸, play for Babaa 爸爸.' If she very good she allow stay in Hotel with me. I manage here. She get spoilt by staff. Too much sweet cake.

He chuckles and takes another sip of cognac.

You must always be polite, even when winning. Insist pay for opponent drink, or he think heart cold. Provide only best cognac!

He places the glass and mah-jong 麻將 tile down onto the chest.

Never lose temper if man cannot pay. Tell him no worry. Is OK. Pay back in time.

He quickly picks up the knife on the chest, playful and threatening.

He happy now. Never forget he owe you. After he think well of you. Your reputation stay good. Much better for business, in long term.

He smiles charmingly, toying with the knife. Lights and music change, scene shifts to:

Scene Seven

The silhouette of the Ghost appears, back-lit in a shimmering pool of light. She stands centre upstage, under the headpiece. The Ghost continues the legend of the Clear and Bright Festival 清明節的傳說. She is holding the knife reverently.

GHOST Do you know how it is to be true Thick Face 厚臉, Black Heart practitioner 黑心手? Fear is to man's soul as drop of poison to well of spring water.

The Ghost stabs herself, laughs, then spits on the knife.

When you conceal your will from others, that is Thick. When you impose your will on other, that is Black. The root of Black Heart is the Killer Instinct. All great Emperor had perfect Killer Instinct.

The Ghost runs her finger along the edge of the blade to give the appearance of cutting herself. Then she holds her finger up to lick the wound in a sensual and erotic way.

After Concubine Li 驪姬 drove him out, the Emperor grandson, Chong Er 重耳, go through much hardship with his loyal men. One day they come to remote place. It is wild and uninhabited. Chong Er 重耳, worn out and hungry, can go no further. He collapse to the ground. His loyal men search for long time but find no food. One loyal man, Jie Zitui 介子推, is deeply worried about Chong Er 重耳. He quietly retreat to secluded place…

The Ghost raises the knife and brings it down onto her thigh in a sweeping arc.

…and cut a piece of flesh from his thigh! [*fighting the pain*] Then he cook up bowl of soup with his flesh and take soup to Chong Er 重耳 in his hand. [*drops the knife*]

The Ghost stretches her cupped hands out to the audience as an offering of her flesh. The knife stays on the floor where it fell, ready for the next scene. Lights and music change:

Scene Eight

Tiananmen Square, June 3, 1989, 10 P.M.
  The hotel room. Jackie paces, looking out the window. She speaks directly to the audience.

JACKIE [*anxiously*] They've come from all directions, since 6 o'clock tonight. They don't look friendly. They've got assault rifles. Convoys. That's what Paul said—military convoys. [*pause*] God, where is he? [*reassuring*] I'm sure he'll be all right. Never gone out with a boy like him. A real sweetie though. [*laughs*] My mother can't stand Chinese men, and she's Chinese!

She reads the letter, imitating Abbie.

'Your father wants to know how many letters you've sent me. I think you'd better write him more. He's worried about you, Jackie, and I really don't know about you and this Paul. You know, Chinese men, they don't make good lovers, they only care about money 錢 and their bodies…they're like little girls!' [*incredulous*] Chinese men don't make good lovers? What about pakeha ones? 'Not trust guilo 鬼佬 as far as throw him,' says Paw paw 婆婆. And what does my mother do? She married one. And what'd he do? He left her. [*recalls*] They all turned up for my farewell dinner…God what a night! It started off OK—except for Paw paw 婆婆 hissing in my ear 'Guilo bring guipo 鬼佬帶來了鬼婆!' We're in this restaurant. All dressed up. Sitting in a big circle. Very polite. Mum on one side, Paw paw 婆婆 on the other. Across the table Janet and Dad. Janet—she's not much older than me. So there we are, sitting round smiling…bit like chimpanzees. They grimace when they're frightened. 'The little girl's grown up. Time for the big O.E.' Dad's got his home video, sticking the camera in my face! Then he shoves it right onto Paw paw 婆婆: 'Smile to the camera Mamee 媽媽.' First she hisses at him. 'Not call me Mamee 媽媽,' but it's like he's got a death wish or something. 'Go on Mamee 媽媽, talk to the little birdie. Tell us what you think about Jackie going away…Janet wants to know too, don't you, Janet?' That was it!

Jackie picks up the knife from the floor.

Paw paw 婆婆 starts waving this knife around. 'You bring shame to Abbie! I kill you, I kill you!!' Next thing there's plates and glasses flying everywhere, and I'm holding on to her trying to get the knife! I tell you for a sixty-eight-year-old she's got a hell of a grip! And there's Janet. White as a ghost. Mumbles some excuse and scarpers. Flees the scene.

Jackie laughs, placing the knife on the chest.

Poor Dad! Some farewell…Even offered to foot the bill for the breakages.

Lights and music change, scene shifts to:

Scene Nine

Wellington, June 1989.

   Abbie's sitting room, the moment following the end of her last scene. Abbie continues speaking into her dictaphone to Jackie, who is in China.

ABBIE [*laughs*] The trouble with us Chinese is that we're supposed to be inscrutable—you never know what we're thinking, what we're going to do next. When I was sixteen I ran away from home. And your grandfather tracked me down. I was staying with my pakeha girl-friend, Charlene. Babaa爸爸 had this man with him, a market gardener. He knew I hated him. He was like a peasant. The kind that blew his [*disgust*] snot onto his shirt sleeve! Brought him anyway. Like back-up. Poor Charlene. She opened the door and Babaa爸爸 just stormed in. [*incredulous*] Spat in my face! Then he hugged me. The first time he'd touched me since I was little. [*pause, then with difficulty*] He started to cry. Actually crying…He was going on about how I was a…his little baby girl, his piano baby. I had to stand there letting him hold me, while this stupid man, this stupid peasant said things to me. Hissed at me. How…how ungrateful! You bring shame!…recriminations…things.

Abbie recovers herself, laughing, embarrassed.

Don't know why I'm telling you this…I—Damn!

Abbie turns off the dictaphone, disconcerted.

Lawyer's office…Wellington, 1959…I was so young.

Lights and music change, scene shifts to:

Scene Ten

Wellington, 1959.
   Abbie is speaking to her lawyer. She directs her speech out to the audience.

ABBIE My mother calls me a slut. You don't believe me, do you? Yes, my own mother! [*pause*] Yes, my parents are respectable, law abiding citizens but…I came to you Mr Wrightson because you're Charlene's father. She said you could help. Everyone says you're a great lawyer…I'm aware that this doesn't look good for the community but I need protection…Yes, I'm twenty-one now…No, my father doesn't hit me frequently. Bruises?! No…It's not quite like that…it's more subtle…He threatens me. He wants to know everything. Who I see, what I do…I don't want to stir up trouble. [*frustrated*] No, I can't talk to anyone else. It's a small community. They all think my parents are—honourable… It'll bring shame to…I want to leave. Please can you speak to them? I'm old enough to live my own life…I want to marry Nigel. I don't care that he's white. [*pause*] Sorry…but if my father finds out I'm telling you this…I just want to be free!

Abbie suddenly looks to the side, shocked.

Babaa爸爸?!—What are you doing here? No…no!!

She falls back as if struck.

Lights and music change, scene shifts to:

Scene Eleven

The silhouette of the Ghost appears, back-lit in a shimmering pool of light. She continues the legend. Peking Opera sounds swell around her.

GHOST Poverty窮 is the greatest violence. The Chinese character for money錢 is compose of three symbol. One is gold. The other two represent spear. The character for poverty窮 is also compose of three symbol. The symbol depict a man standing at the bottom of pit, bent as if under great burden.

> *The Ghost becomes Chong Er重耳, her hands are outstretched as before, she devours the soup.*

> Chong Er重耳 devoured his soup ravenously. Recovering his strength [*holds hand out*]…he ask his men, 'Where did meat come from?' The men looked at Jie Zitui介子推, his gown is stain with blood. Chong Er重耳 so happy he embrace Jie Zitui介子推…'What shall I do to repay you?' Jie Zitui介子推 reply, 'You have taste the full bitterness of the people through this exile. I wish you only be King clear and bright in future.'

Lights and music change, scene shifts to:

Scene Twelve

Hong Kong, 1941.

   Sudden dramatic darkness and exploding sounds, a scream. Sounds of the approaching Japanese invasion without. As the lights come up Paw paw婆婆 is clutching Abbie (the mock-up baby in swaddling) who is only a few months old. She is panicking, trying to stop Abbie's crying while making the motions of packing, using the long red cloths as if one were a sack and the others were items of clothing. She has misplaced her precious family heirloom, the gold chain and locket. Paw paw婆婆 searches desperately while directing her speech to the baby. At the end of the scene we find the heirloom has been in her pocket all along.

PAW PAW Good luck, is what you need. A lot of it. How I suppose to get you out? Not even Kuomintang國民党 save us now.

She stops packing to search for the gold.

It all because of you! My husband say I not go to New Zealand unless I bring you. Here we are, stuck in Hong Kong and Japanese invasion! All because of you! Abbie, Abbie—what stupid name for baby! [*to herself*] Was not safe before. So hide it again. I put in here I know. 1941—not good year. Year of Snake 蛇年! No wonder there so much trouble. War everywhere. I put it—where? Where?! [*screams*] Shut up! You lucky you bless with me. [*pause*] He always have soft spot for your mother, Lady Li 驪夫人. She was nothing, nothing but concubine! I am first wife, me!

She now directs her venom at baby Abbie.

Wishee you die with her, wishee she jump down well with you inside her stomach! Till na ma 操你媽!!

She lunges for the baby's throat but stops short, breathing heavily.

Never mind. You help me work in fruit shop.

She begins her search for the locket again.

Lucky you bless with me. If leave you here, maybe Japanese man eat you. That what Ma say. Japanese men like eat baby. You lucky I take you. Yes.

The sound of approaching gunfire gets louder, as do Abbie's cries. Paw paw 婆婆 is distracted as she hurries through belongings, tossing things everywhere, looking for her gold locket.

Maybe I send you for school, maybe. Take my son Cyril. And you. [*angry*] Cyril cry for his father. He good boy. He only little. My husband not need hit him so hard. I give him son but he like you more because you hers. Shut up!…Can't find it! You repay me. Look after me and Babaa 爸爸. Repay debt. Be good daughter. Least I can walk. Not like some women. With golden lily feet. Japanese probably rape them. Me! I can run!

She finds her gold, hugely relieved.

Oh! Yes…Daw geh! Daw geh! Now we go…

She searches for a new place to hide the gold.

Where they not find?

She places the gold into the baby's napkin.

Maybe they not look for it in here. Mix blessing. Story of my life. Mix blessing.

She suddenly remembers Cyril, her son, and the amah 阿媽, *and calls out to them, off-stage.*

Cyril? Cyril! Amah 阿媽! Come. Quick!

Lights and music change, end act one.

Act Two

Scene One _____

Wellington, 1959, Nigel's student flat.
  Abbie is arguing with Paw paw 婆婆 *over the telephone.*

ABBIE I'm not coming home…I'm not coming home. I'm going to live…[*suspicious*]…Yes, I am at Nigel's flat…I'm not coming…Listen, Mamee 媽媽…He's not a Communist for God's sake, he's a student! It's 1959, Mamee 媽媽, things are different…It's not like that…Nigel's not that sort of person! Mamee 媽媽…Ma…listen to…Mamee 媽媽, listen to me, we're getting…We're getting married!…Mamee 媽媽? [*mutters*] I couldn't feel more lucid actually…No…lucid's not a drug—oh never mind. Aunty Ying 瑛阿姨 came around…Aunty Ying 瑛阿姨! She was being insufferable…No I'm not swearing…Nigel says the Chinese community are frightened…from years of [*trails off*] oppressions…what? [*shocked silence*] No!…No!!

  Paw paw 婆婆 *hangs up on the other end. Abbie places the receiver down, fuming.*

OK—Fine!

Lights and music change, scene shifts to:

Scene Two _____

The Ghost is centre upstage, under the headpiece.

GHOST Nineteen years after his exile Chong Er 重耳 become Emperor of China.

After ascend throne, he confer title and award to meritorious official who follow him in exile, only to forget Jie Zitui 介子推. Many people angry at injustice done to Jie, advise him to see Chong Er 重耳 ask for reward. Jie Zitui 介子推 however refuse contend for merit. Instead, he quietly got things ready, went to Mianshang Mountain 綿上山 to live in seclusion, carrying his old mother upon his back.

Lights and music change, scene shifts to:

Scene Three

Wellington, 1959, the Leung family kitchen.

Paw paw婆婆 is arguing with young Abbie over the telephone. She breaks in and out of English and Cantonese. On the chest is the rice bowl with chopsticks.

PAW PAW [*polite*] Abbie?…Ah. You think so? You think maybe you stay with him? [*pause*] You run away now?…Ah, but you at his place?…Oh do not bother on behalf of us. We just silly old Chinese people. [*cold*] Just wait till Babaa 爸爸 find out! You stupid girl. Abbie—a guilo 鬼佬! [*laughs*] With no money 錢. Aiyee哎呀! A Communist too, eh? Probably he is! You give us bad name. Not care about family?…Selfish child. We send you to good school. What you do for us, eh? You thanking us by sleeping with guilo 鬼佬! You so stupid. He leave you. I know. He leave you for other white girl. [*shocked pause*] You mahlee…You mahlee?!…You want I die? You must be outa your mind!…Lucid? Now you tell me you on drug too? I curse you…What you say? Who?…Why you swearing about at Aunty Ying?…Is rubbish!…See! Communist!…All guilo 鬼佬 want is…is…to make fuck with you. You think he wanna mahlee you? You got be choking! He mahlee you for our money 錢 that all! Don't think you can put your face round here! You not come home—no, no! Never come home now! You are…are…slut! [*spits*] See Mung Nui 死懵女! [*tries to compose herself*] Abbie, you come back or I tell Babaa 爸爸. He cut you allowance! You leave—got no money 錢—you die, starve to death! [*tearful*] All my children so selfish. Not care how hard they make my life! [*suddenly cold*] I tell Babaa 爸爸! He get you, give you proper beating! [*venomous*] Proper beating!

Paw paw婆婆 hangs up on Abbie, fumes for a moment then picks up her bowl of rice and begins to eat, calming herself.

It dark when I wake. Put on woollen singlet. Corset. Thick stocking. Keep leg warm. Bloomer. Old cheongsam老長衫. Put on my sock. Three pair these day. Black glove, no finger. Better for pick up fruit. Go downstair and open shop. First customer Mr Jone. He always come too early—complain service slow. I tell him. Mr Jone 7 o'clock we open shop. Then Mr Jone you buy banana for breakfast. I even offer deliver. But he bit crazy. Anyway he say to me 'Have nice day' and I give him banana. [*pause*] When children little, next door Parker kid rude to Cyril. Cyril just little boy then. He good boy. This Parker kid little shit. He say to Cyril, 'Ching chong China man, eatee doggie in fry pan!' Punch Cyril! It very hard for Cyril. He not allow fight back. Give us bad name. [*pause*] Guilo 鬼佬 call us 'alien.' Say we pay one hundred pound or not come. It take long time save, I sell family gold, just to come! Leave Amah 阿媽 behind. Cyril cry for Amah 阿媽 when we get on big boat. He want her come too. Everything different here. No Amah 阿媽 look after children… [*pause*] New Zealand government not charge anyone else fee but Chinese. They let us in New Zealand, say we be good and only stay two year. Until war over. Then we all go home. Back to China…

[*angry*] Why we go back when Japanese everywhere?!!

She pauses to eat some rice.

We ate pigeon from park one day. Why not? Maybe I shoulda kill next-door Parker dog. One day stupid mutt got one of my chicken. Mr Parker not even say sorry. [*pause*]

Better I not. Make government unhappy—if I eat neighbour dog. Guilos 鬼佬! So stupid! We only people with sense. If you hungry just whistle and it come. No need hunt or fuss! [*pause*] And him. Mr Parker. He no better than a dog far as I can see. Like my husband. Stupid man. Always drinking and screaming at wife. My husband spend too long with guilo 鬼佬. Gone to his head. My husband say, 'come over, come over,' writing letter. I in Hong Kong with Japanese invasion, he say, 'Come over, plenty of money 錢 here for family. Business good.' What business? Stupid shit! No money 錢 because he spend it all on himself at stupid hotel on stupid mah-jong 麻將, and the woman. [*warily*] I know he has her. This not home. Not China. He think he can be married more than one wife. They arrest him. If he try marry another I leave him. He think I not know but I do. I seen him. Think I not know. I just say nothing. [*frustrated*] One day he want I give school money 錢. No way! Our children gotta go. I want Cyril be doctor, one day. Abbie play piano. Good husband want her if she go good school. It gotta be that way. I tell him. He say no. Kid work for business first. He start yelling. He want money 錢 bad. For debt. [*defeated*] For long time I hold my tongue. [*defiantly*] Then I tell him. I say No. No more for mah-jong 麻將. No more take, take, take. He say I 'bitch' or something. Say I be good to him or he go. [*with great strength*] Sure. He go. He got nothing. I work. My business.

*Paw paw*婆婆 *places her bowl and chopsticks on the chest, rubbing her sore back. Lights and music change, scene shifts to:*

Scene Four

Wellington, June 1989.
   Abbie in her sitting room, continues her letter to Jackie.

ABBIE A cat's skeleton in the backyard!—Rain's been coming down in buckets! Typical for Wellington. Neighbour's backyard slid down the hill onto my pathway and there it was. I thought it was a dead person at first, got such a fright.

She laughs, then pauses.

It reminded me of old Aunty Ying's 瑛阿姨 tales about the bones. She said they were on this ship. What was it called? [*recalls*] The *Ventnor*…Went down off the Hokianga, sometime around 1900. She insisted it was carrying all these exhumed bones of old Chinese miners. [*pause*] Imagine hundreds of bodies on a ship—yuk, creepy. Anyway, Aunty said it sank because of the fighting. [*laughs*] She'd get all worked up when she'd tell me about it. Apparently it was all the Hoy clan's fault, trying to pick a fight with our clan. Aunty reckons if the Hoys weren't so greedy then the ghosts wouldn't have died a second death. The ghosts had a scrap! They had a big ghost punch-up and knocked a hole in the side of the boat! Old grudges…

She laughs at first, then her mood changes as she thinks of Paw paw 婆婆. *She stops the dictaphone, placing it back on the chest.*

I wish…I wish I could understand you, Mamee媽媽. And I wonder why I hate you sometimes. Guilo 鬼佬 men really don't make good lovers. You were right after all. But neither do our own flesh and blood. I'd rather have a tall white hairy man with a fickle temperament than marry someone like my father!…A sinking ship. [*laughs*] God, I used to get so frustrated with Nigel. He'd sit on the loo for hours playing correspondence chess. I'd stand shouting at the door, 'If our home were a sinking ship…!' [*pauses*] That photograph. The whole of Marsden Girls. Prissy little uniforms. Hung on the toilet wall for years. Went all yellow and mildewed from age. I'd sit on the loo and stare at myself as a child. There I sat, smack bang in the middle of all those white faces. The only coloured one. A five-year-old.

[*pause*] I remember…They took that photo the day after our swimming lesson…Funny, I never smiled then. [*dreamily*] Wellington, 1946. The schoolteacher calls Mamee媽媽 on the new telephone.

Explaining that I need togs. Takes a while, since neither Paw paw婆婆 nor I speak good English. Swimming day arrives—I'm shocked at the sight of so many nude white girls! I've never seen anything like it. I don't want to undress in front of them. All the other girls line up, laughing. Lots of noise. The teacher pushes me into line...[*gasps in wonder*] The water looked lovely. All blue and sparkly. The girls' heads bobbing up and down. It's magic. It must be magic. So I just step in.

Abbie closes her eyes, smiling. There is a moment's silence. Then she opens her eyes, wide with wonder.

Don't know what's happening to me. The noises...all muffled, dislocated. All those white girlie legs. So much thrashing nakedness. Open my mouth to call out, to breathe...[*gulps, begins to panic*] I'm moving...slow motion...like a dream. Clumsy, grasping at one girl, she pushes me away...I'm sinking...Some steps, I can see some steps ...Can't breathe...Crawling...Can't breathe...crawling towards them...

Abbie is suddenly gasping and spluttering. She tries to compose herself, shaking.

The teachers...they don't notice me, no one notices me...Just sitting there, trying to be quiet...but my teeth are chattering. [*giggles nervously*] Shh—shh—I have the tremors, sitting trying not to be noticed...Thinking—sh—shh! shh!

Abbie melts into the darkness. Lights and music change, scene shifts to:

Scene Five

Hotel Selwyn, 1949.
  Gung gung 公公 is holding his glass of cognac.

GUNG GUNG [*chuckles*] Never play against a pregnant woman! My number four concubine四妾, Lady Li 驪夫人, very pretty. In mah-jong 麻將, to catch moon from bottom of sea, must always take last tile, in last round. Lady Li 驪夫人 is pregnant when she play against us. [*chuckles again*] She ah, how you say?...Ahh! Win great victory!

He laughs, then stops and a tender look of great sadness comes over his face.

She look like this...when she die. Like the moon under the sea. Her face float up from bottom of well, like moon on the water...Lady Li 驪夫人...

Lights and music change, scene shifts to:

Scene Six

Tiananmen Square, June 3, 1989.
   The hotel room at midnight. Jackie is hurriedly preparing to leave.

JACKIE Anyway Mum, I've gotta run, said I'd meet Paul in the Square 天安門廣場.

> *She pauses briefly to stare out the venetian blinds. The scene is shocking. She looks back at the audience trying to cover her fear.*

> Promise I won't get into trouble. Maybe China's almost ready. By the way, you'll be pleased to know. Paul and I are leaving for Hong Kong in the next couple of days. Things are coming to a close, looks like the protest is finally over. [*insisting*] Everything's fine. Anyway. Love you heaps Mum—give everybody big kisses from me. Jackie.

Lights and music change, scene shifts to:

Scene Seven

Wellington, 1968.
   An older Paw paw婆婆 is holding her granddaughter Jackie as a baby. She is warm and loving. As she speaks she wraps the soft white baby's blanket around the child, and smiles warmly. Paw paw婆婆 is tired from work, so occasionally she nurses a sore back.

PAW PAW Good little Jackieleen. Beautiful baby. Paw paw婆婆 love little Jackie. Never you mind you got white Daddy. You still most beautiful granddaughter to Paw paw婆婆.

> *She holds up the gold chain and locket.*

> For you. It is. Very special. From my mother to me to…to baby Jackieleen. Yes. Make me very happy to see you have this. Gold! Is good luck.

> *She pulls the chain away, slightly alarmed.*

> Ah, I not give it you now Jackieleen. You might eat. I give it you when you big enough. You can have everything from me. Special little granddaughter to Paw paw婆婆.

> *She shuffles to the chair and seats herself comfortably, soothing the child.*

1968. [*frowning*] Born in Year of Monkey 屬猴. [*smiles*] Very smart. Is all right. You not worry. Is summer so you never hungry in lifetime.

She inspects the child, delighted.

Ahh. Fat ear lobe is good too. Jackieleen have very beautiful ear lobe. Mean much good food. Never mind you girl. That OK nowaday. You lucky not born in China, ah? Back in old day you were bad luck. First born must always be boy. But not here, ah? [*pause*] Abbie and Cyril say I should go to China. Back home. [*sadness*] What home? Is no one left. [*shakes it off*] Ah! I teach you everything when you big. [*laughs, crooning*] There once famous man called Jie Zitui 介子推. He famous because he cut off flesh and cook in soup for King when King starving. Jie Zitui die because King want make him someone he not like. Make him official.

She stands and places the child on the chair carefully with the gold chain next to it, nursing her sore back. She continues to direct the story to the child.

He carry his old mother with him all the way. Even die with her. When they find body under willow tree, he write note in own blood. Say, 'I cut off my flesh to dedicate you my utter devotion, I wish only my King always be clear and bright. [*with great tenderness*] If you bear me in mind, make self-examination whenever you recollect me.'

Lights and music change, scene shifts to:

Scene Eight

Wellington, June 1989.

   Karori cemetery. Abbie moves downstage to the white rose. She kneels by the graveside of her mother. Jackie does not yet know of Paw paw's 婆婆 death. Abbie is trying to quell conflicting emotions as she picks up the rose.

ABBIE Tell me something, Mamee 媽媽. Cyril gets pissed off because you wrote a will. Fifteen years ago you wrote a will. You think you're gonna die tomorrow and fifteen years later... [*laughs*] All your gold goes to Jackie. [*gentle*] Yes, that's right, the oldest granddaughter, just like tradition. Only, Cyril gets pissed off. He gets pissed off and says to me, 'You're not even one of us.'

She pauses, regarding the rose in her hands, then she places it by the headstone and takes a deep breath.

Fifty years ago you brought a little baby girl from China. Everybody assumed she was yours, even the little girl. As she grew up, she assumed lots of things. Like your right to…to…to be the kind of a mother that you were…[*laughs*] You used to make me recite the Chinese book四書! I was six. I was only six, for Christ's sake. Standing at the dinner table. Over and over. I didn't understand a word of it. No, but you checked that I had every word right. And if I got one wrong! [*pause*] Good way for me to lose weight, Mamee媽媽. Oh yes. I stayed nice and slim for those cheongsams長衫. They fitted like a glove. Like a glove. And I wore them. A bright-coloured bird. All that expensive plumage to attract a husband. [*laughs*] Only, I started to enjoy the effect. I was exotic. Oh yes. By the time I was eighteen I had all the boys at university following me—just whistle and they'd come. Your daughter the whore. [*pause*] Sorry, Mamee媽媽. No rich Chinese businessmen there—all the Chinese boys ran away. They were terrified of you. Old dragon lady! [*laughs, close to tears*] I was so lonely. You took everyone…But not Jackie. You couldn't have Jackie. She was mine. For the first time. Something of mine.

She gasps, remembering that Jackie does not yet know of Paw paw's 婆婆 death.

She doesn't even know you're dead. [*angry*] No! Don't you start nagging at me, we all tried to contact her. She'll find out soon enough—Oh just shut up!

Abbie is momentarily embarrassed by her outburst.

Mamee媽媽…Why?…You wouldn't even say it. Not even on your death bed…You just lay there, your eyes glazing up, staring at me and you went on and on about some…[*laughs painfully*] some Lady Li's麗夫人 shrimp dumplings…Shrimp fucking dumplings! [*pause*] You would never say it, that you were not my mother…[*through tears, tenderly*] Mamee媽媽…I don't care about the gold. All I want is the truth.

As Abbie reaches for the rose on the floor, the lights change. Scene shifts to:

Scene Nine

The streets of Beijing, Tiananmen Square, June 4, 1989, 2 A.M.
    Shouting, a burst of gunfire, then eerie quiet. Suddenly we see Jackie, knocked and jostled by the huge crowd. She staggers to her feet, dazed and confused.

JACKIE What the…Paul?…Paul? Where are you?

> *Suddenly she is blinded by the glare of tank lights, and then what she sees horrifies her.*

> It's a sea out here…so many people…Paul?…No…let me go…I must get to him…No!…Oh Jesus, God no…please don't hurt him…[*screaming*] Paul!…Paul!!

Blackout. Sounds of protests and BBC news coverage swell in the darkness then fade to an echo.

Scene Ten

> *The Ghost, centre upstage, under the headpiece. She is calling tenderly to the baby on the chair.*

GHOST Abbie…Abbie, who is your mamee? Abbie…

> *She moves as if she is floating, towards the child.*

> And the Mianshang Mountain 綿上山 was very high with dense forest and difficult pass. When Emperor Chong Er 重耳 realise his neglect he make personal call to Jie Zitui's 介子推 house only to find the door is lock. Jie was unwilling become official and went to mountain top, carrying his mother on his back.

> *She gathers the baby in her arms, moving back towards the headpiece. As she does this the red backdrop lights up as if on fire.*

> Chong Er 重耳 order forest be burn to smoke Jie out. Soaring fire immediately spread from three sides of mountain, burning over all Mianshang, yet not a shadow of Jie was found. When fire went out, people find Jie dead sitting under old willow tree, his mother still on his back. Seeing this, all the people felt unbearable painful and nearly cry their heart out.

> *She kisses the child, then she softly hums a lullaby and tenderly rocks the swaddled baby in her arms.*

Lights and music fade.

from Cat's Eye in a Splintered Mirror ⎯⎯⎯⎯⎯⎯⎯⎯⎯⎯⎯⎯⎯⎯⎯

for Merril

11

You go down on one knee, an antelope enters the valley
Deep from golden wheat fields comes the chime of

evening prayer. Fruit hang down in tandem, ripe
kernels popping

The slender neck of a water bird glistens
damp. Dark, the fringes of a city

glow with lamplight. White towers
tilt farther when you stand up suddenly

A gray badger screams, the night sky brightens
Last one to sleep is happiest

The night I take leave of leaves me
nothing to do come day

Pay attention to details. The ocean shivers snow-
whitely by a dark dune it washes

Tropical grass, once dense, is now
disappearing. Sightseers stand in fog

Three men singing a work song
plod down black rock

tugging a yellow wooden boat
Another taller snow-white wave

rolls over their heads in the dark
I write love poems, idling my life away

12

Layer by layer you disappear into
the crystal of memory. The mountain path shrinks
in dense fog. Pine nuts falling in the nearby

wood deepen the descent into the canyon
People of two realities talk; all night long
the surge is loud and incessant

the space between us more clearly defined
We head each in his own direction, moving apart
Now a derelict throws a great hunk of

wood onto the fire. Night birds
fly a straight course. While we say
nothing, countless black sea crabs crawl eagerly

from white foam onto the
glistening sand. The night sky roars
close to a hand on its own

You are fading into deeper fog, brightest
parts gone. The horse blanketed in
blue follows the slant of shadows

Short-legged coyotes howl
all night long at the end of this vast low-lying
southward land. In the palms of my hands

remains still the feel of breasts
young, sturdy, pointed

13

Poetry I write for you carries the
fragrance of a tree-full of white flowers
The visitor departs when the scent

is sweetest, a fox disappears from the deep valley
A discarded red barn
bending its neck in June looks like you

when you are reading in the back yard
on weekends. While you are having a
nap a traveler arrives

in the city. A blurred little bird
flies towards the bell tower pinnacle. Ebb tide
floats out of town the men demanding to

express their emotions. In a tropical sunset
drug addicts, bodies stiff, gaze merrily
towards immeasurable sea

As you close this book of poems, these seasonal
flowers send forth sweetest fragrance

Translation by Hu Qian and Keith Waldrop

STEPHAN TORRE

Three Poems

REFERRAL

Empty yourself, my Buddhist
friend urged, let the bull thistle
blow out of the naked orchard,
rasp and auger down through
your pulpy lungs and bacon.

Sweaty old latigo tightens
around the center of this
fleshy bag of intentions, nervous
duffel of garlic and gingerroot, wobbly
stump full of pitch, rum, gratitude,
spikes and beetle holes, hungry
bag of man.

It's gonna take some time
for the porcupine waddling
through pine duff to settle
for a burnt hollow log, or the punky
house Bluebear ripped
open for dessert

and a dusty satori. Gonna
take some time to shake out
all the bluetooth grog, gringo salsa,
Berkeley grinds and shards
of broken Cartesian mirror.
Whatever agitation
you ascribe to this porky

pine-eating wanderer,
don't mistake him
for the blackjack dealer,
coon in a culvert,
or the weasel slipping
through a rusty pipe

for a mouthful of rat.
Temple server and lotus
seeker, listen:
behind his black lips
is a glowing cud of amber.

FORD

If you have ever slid down into the last
purpling light of November from a pine snag
or juniper, like a chicken hawk or magpie, sleek
in your russet vest or black and white cocktail suit,
arrogant and fat with roadkill or hot rabbit heart;
ever cruised down the omnivorous dusk from lava-cracked sky
or abandoned barn rafters, over alkali swales, tufa,
sage, coyote tails, bitterbrush, rattler fangs, the powdering
bones of cattle and buckaroo geldings—like señor magpie,
quick butler of solitudes, you would know
why an old pickup full of diesel might even
tempt a Buddha.

UNDER THE BADGER'S NOSE, LATE JANUARY

If the fang of moon
at your elbow, cutting ice and lava
from a winter rim rock night,

or the yellowing plastic can
of twelve-volt light with dead bugs
above your balding head in the trailer;

whether another ham and jack
Cartesian sandwich, or simply
a hard-boiled Nietzschean

or Buddhist egg
to suck on with a shot
of pepper and tequila,

either way you gulp
down the liquors of solitude
this light on your wrist

is always ample and exquisite
for the certain feast you have
dug for and deserved.

Still Center

Heaven around earth
earth around sun
sun around stars
stars around universe
universe around time
time around death
death around you

Love around heart
heart around hope
hope around mind
love heart hope mind
love around you

death still to come
still the heart and mind
death mind heart hope
hope around you

love around you
death around you
love death
heart hope mind
sun stars sky
earth heaven time

universe around mind
mind around heart
heart around love
love around death
love around death

love around you
Māhealani
love around you

IONA

A portfolio of

photographs by

Sergio Goes

Angels in America: on Hallmark cards, on network TV, on Broadway. And in Hawai'i: angels (harder to believe, but believe it) on the streets, at the mall, in hospices and prisons.

In Iona's *The Mythology of Angels,* celestial beings are the spiritual manifestations of cultures all over the world. The Iona dancers are an ethnic mix, fleshly, intensely physical, moving always in awareness of the dancing body as part of the energy of the universe. Preparation for performance takes them through motionless meditation to boundless improvisation to endless repetitions that burn choreography into muscle memory. On top of the day job, hour upon week of rehearsal in starving-artist studios. Mottled mirrors. Props piled in discard. A shopping bag of knee pads for the unforgiving floor. Sweat. Cramps. Bruises. Pulled muscles. Shared wisdom from the East, specifics for pain: Tiger Balm, Kwan Loong. And shared laying-on of knowledgeable healing hands. They fall with each other, they lift each other up. A company of dancers. On stage in *The Mythology of Angels* they take wing, they are silver and they soar.

Dance is their liberation. Around them they see people condemned, forbidden to soar, behind prison bars, or caged in an ageing body, or trapped in a fearful mind, or just caught in the heavy traffic of a workaday world grinding slowly and clashingly through the gears of life. If angels appear, what might follow?

GAVAN DAWS

CONTEMPORARY DANCE THEATRE

*Seeing and seen
through the eyes of
Iona; silvered flesh
rising to spirit*

Seeking and finding; an
Iona angel enters

Reaching and touching,
giving and receiving,
offering and accepting

There is a world beyond
the concrete; Iona's
angel looks to the light

Grace translated;
an unpredicted angel
appears and attends

LUO YING

Three Poems

THE SNOW IS A SOFT AND GENTLE FOREST

We pass through the snow
Far away, the war is progressing
Death, blind in both eyes
Touches our feet
Darling, your hands are so cold
Secrets are growing in your eyes
Flowers given you by others are growing
But that's a mistake. Mistake. It wears a mask, blocking our way
It ties us up together with a slender cord
Carving a scar over our hearts as a sign
And it occurs to both of us that someone is dying at this very moment
The shadow of Death is spreading
We try wearing our lives inside out
At least they look newer that way
Final words, they're neither old nor new
And we wear them on our bodies too
And then we walk towards the tunnel
The sound of gunshots says the slaughter is still going on
The snow is weaving time
And the snow continues as well
We pass through the soft and gentle forest of snow
Death won't stain the snow black
It can't stain today or tomorrow black
In the narrow, narrow space inside my white, white heart
You lie, deep in sleep
You're smiling
You see me
When the sun, like a remark, brief and to the point
Makes its hesitant ascent

Out of the cold, cold air
Out of Death's loose black robes
We pass through the snow
We move across the slope of the clock
We pass through the small river of time
We and the snow embrace, we and Death embrace
We and the past, and the past before the past
Embrace
Sounds fade away into silence like cannon fodder
We and so many story lines, so many loves
We brush past them and continue on our way

ANTS

Ants, their clans
Lined up in rows, character after character, into a sequence of poems
The sounds of love linger, echoing back
They murmur among themselves, droning and humming underground
Surging throngs
Tonight in my dreams
Compose songs
And write poems

DAYLILY'S JOURNEY

1

voice
calling out to voice
the hours never come home
mother rides the boat alone
in the river of glittering stars
she has washed and dried
homecoming story lines time and again
the boat drifts along
drifts into the line
of the figure made by wild geese flying homeward

2

mother's embroidered shoes
slightly damp

the tears she cried when she was young
mother
she stubbornly turns to face the wall
reading the past and the past that came before the past
without a word
catching a ride on a *wutong* leaf
under the hollow of a bow-shaped bridge
we meet up
with an autumn long since vanished
and me, before I was born

3

a dark corner of a wall
crickets say that the sun is too far and the cold is too near
following the cracks between the brickwork
the spirit world
is too distant and too close
from here
mother takes her footsteps, swift and light like dried leaves
and puts them away in a chest of drawers
takes the moth-eaten but perfectly round moonlight
and gently moves it to a space beside her pillow
neither speaking nor awake, nor alive
mother
is the well in front of the door
a stone inside the well

4

how can one refuse
a gentle breeze
how can one refuse
a sparrow's approaching flight
mother always flies
without direction, without a way back
she's always flying
scattering bits of feather-shaped
love, non-love, nostalgia, non-nostalgia
mother, she is light and airy, soft and gentle
in the mist where moonlight and candlelight enhance each other
lightly and almost soundlessly
carrying these burnt words
and the story the words can only tell confusedly
reluctantly

she flies, and keeps
flying

5

umbrellas, surrounded by umbrellas
funeral umbrellas are a sad grove of trees
black umbrella black umbrella black umbrella
tears flow down the hillsides of sloping umbrellas
death
did it rehearse?
so smoothly
mother has come to the lowest layer of the earth
a black butterfly
follows her
alights on her eyelashes
mother's face
is quivering, is trembling
and completely dried
of any traces of tears

Translations by Andrea Lingenfelter

Five Poems

NATURAL SCIENCE TEACHER

Finally I spy that bundle of light, slowly flowing into the woods. Like a silent stream, leaving a waterfall, myriad specks of dust, like spores, float among the beams, exploring, or aimlessly wander off.

They enter the woods. There's a child fascinated by insects, going on and on about plants with me. There's a youngster who loves climbing mountains and fording streams, who will someday trace every range I've crossed. As for that girl who writes like a poem, she's never grown up, still that same likeness of an eleven-year old I dote on.

They'll come across my death, in different places. It might be like the shards of a beetle shell, or possibly a rotting, withered tree.

And, by chance, they'll encounter my birth, a kind of essence even more concrete than tender shoots and new leaves, sitting by their side in lonesome moments.

They continue going into the woods. Inside my aged sea-turtle's body they squirm about, vexing me, tiring me, harassing me. It's always been my living question mark, my uncertainty.

ONE SUNNY WINTER MORNING

Owing to the ravages of life,
Blissful travels, and a maturity born of felicity,
I've acquired the disposition of a frog
Heavy-lidded blurry vision
Plodding vague mouthfuls of slurred words
Only savoring delicacies
Taste refined to the snatching of a passing mosquito

Until a great cluster of ferns luxuriantly grows
The deepest recesses of my mind naturally so sodden
And consequently mold-encrusted that
All their former depravity and glory
Are thoroughly ensconced
And completely decay into sediment

CENTRAL RANGES OF BEAR CUB LAHEYUAN

In the night, firelight deepens wrinkles
Eye sockets fall into shadow as well, concealing
A glimmer denser than pity
You squat on your slackened backpack
Only some maize left roasting on the grate
That's tonight's and a lifetime's provisions

At dawn you'll be like a Sambar passing
    through a forest of pine needles
Catching the solemn whisper of dangling
    songluo
A middle-aged, white-haired Shikano
    Tadao traveled just this way
From childhood he entrusted his soul to
    Taiwan
One man bearing the 1930s, visiting Snow
    Mountain seven times
You also want to set out across a mountain
    ridge without a return path
Leaving no descendants, only an isolated
    squat shadow
Letting your skull roll down the pebbled
    slopes

songluo: a lichen (Usnea longissima) commonly called old man's beard, often found hanging from the tips of tree branches

That's a camphor tree, Chinese juniper, hemlock
    spruce—one by one they disappear en masse
Four hundred years of unease
All that survives is this chill stretch of tranquility
Tears roll off the tip of your nose
Onto the raging flames of your dreams
The life of one naturalist
Lonely, so lonely
Let the nutcracker scream awake death
Let the stone tiger gnaw at the flesh
Let the winter night bury the soul

nutcracker: a spotted crow inhabiting tall pine forests

WHAT IS INDESCRIBABLE ABOUT MOUNT INDESCRIBABLE

Perhaps it would be more precise to start with the
    leaf tip of a cold Japanese cedar
That's the moment of contact with the dry edge
    of a long-maned mountain goat's nose
That's an azalea's petals finally dropping
That's an almost intolerably quiet winter dawn
That's a mikado pheasant cock stretching its
    neck to feel the warmth of sunbeams
That's the day when the louse reunion again fills
    the lean-to

I stand on a mountain that maps don't name
Shoulder-to-shoulder with the gaunt clouds,
    with the Han Chinese Xing Tianzheng
Looking upon winter's most remote likeness

Xing Tianzheng: a well-known mountaineer

The vast world of a single Japanese cedar on
    the horizon
An old Taiya man blows on a mouth harp

Taiya: Han Chinese term for one of the aboriginal tribes of Taiwan

My pocket journal has again grown light
The pent-up feelings in my left ventricle have
    once more grown heavy like stones
All my desires turn to ice.

SONG OF THE CHINESE JUNIPER FOREST

Finally, using a myriad of lofty postures
Together with the sky
They towered over the sea of trees

Moreover, separated by the length of a distant gaze
In a skewed world
They kept supporting one another

At that moment everything had matured
There were countless shades of green under the sea of trees
Undulating

Ferns clung to their chests
Groping in the direction of the sun's rays

Orchids clasped their arms
Revealing the glittering brilliance of the forest

Mountain clouds docked on their shoulders
Ready to drift away at dawn

Passing birds found lodgings in their hair
Anticipating the next day's journey

They are a community of elephants
Life inching them upward
Unrestrained for a thousand years
Looking to the depth and vastness of the sky

Looking upon their loftiness
We are travelers who fear solitude but will likely be faced
    with solitude
In a fleeting instant
Incessantly gauging our own insignificance

Translations by Nick Kaldis

Three Poems _____

ISLAND

an ancient cataclysm…

this chunk of rock
jumped from the land to the sea
(carrying the pain of its birth
and the bruises of the thudding)

trees grow there now
bearing fruit, and good people
dwell there

but I won't describe that piece of rock
I'm looking down and watching the completeness of this map…

tilting like a two-winged roc
skimming over every inch of sorrow and joy

I extend my neck, leaving behind
a long, expansive call
reaching back to the very beginning

THE YEARS OF FAMINE

written on a journey, 1996

1

in memory my mother's river
winds around three trees at the mouth of the bay
pressing onward

the woods are overgrown
with a century's brambles

2

are they going east? rivers
no, they're moving south now, or
west, or north
—the flooding has matured
that's the curse of the season
seeking conversation elsewhere

on a road full of misconceptions
every path is an exit

3

even if we close our mouths and refuse to speak
they won't let us keep silent
chasing us with wind from the clouds until we cry out
lashing us with stinging whips of rain until we weep

but all of it happens without a sound
they haven't seen the scars
on our ankles, the backs of our knees, our throats
they're growing (oh, they're growing day by day)
up to our eye sockets…

4

we're running away, running towards
a land without water

like a crushed flute
the sound forsaken because the body is broken

still that's where we're heading, the way station
we're about to reach
only because even ruins can point us towards a certain solemnity

5

we refugees are already on the road
we come upon Qu Yuan
he isn't old and haggard, he's really quite
    ordinary

he's probably already learned—
having offered up loyalty, innocence, and
    zeal
he's left with nothing in the palms of his
    hands, only river water
that slowly rises to reach shoulders, necks,
    the tops of our heads, the sky
only then do we realize that we haven't
    actually learned
how to survive underwater

wicked spray, bright and shining
ripples on the water, flashing chains
that tighten around us
turning into a gang of hellish hedgehogs

only the children, lame in both legs
(oh, those scars, too early and too plentiful)
can come to the train station to bow to and
    praise people
like monks who have suffered a thousand
    hardships
unflinching, they reach out with both arms

their scabbed eyes
so full of life

Qu Yuan was a poet of the third century B.C.E. After being unjustly banished by his king, he committed suicide by drowning himself in a river.

6

and so, we are either too weak
or too strong—simply because
we use the wealth
that comes from children…

Qu Yuan is crying now too
he sees himself through the children's eyes
he isn't old and haggard, it's just that he's in tatters

7

we refugees have already been on the road
for several generations now, familiar faces
fill the ranks
our mothers among them too

mother, help me loosen these bonds
it was there in the keening torrents of the river's upper reaches
that I played the part of a laborer who pulled boats upstream
it was you who gave me this length of rope
and bound me up, so I wouldn't drift away
so I wouldn't shake up the incline of heaven's vault

mother, help me unravel
these confusing symbols and codes
even if the scorching sun has already branded
the scars dividing good and evil
like an invisible order of confiscation
wrapped around my naked body

8

the years of famine, a misunderstood era
were they exiled because they were misunderstood
or were they misunderstood because they went into exile?

(—none of this will ever be cleared up—)

the original pledge was to follow the river downstream
the ancient rooftops have sunk into quarreling and heresy
a brave new world has sprung up
from every direction, violent and lawless

and we have been provoked, abused
strip searched, investigated
stamped, given new identity papers
lighting flames in each other's eyes

but my mother is always silent
only Qu Yuan sternly refuses
and leaves us swiftly

9

the river winds around three trees at the mouth of the bay
something indistinct from the river hangs on the trees
and there are children who have vanished without a trace
my mother gets older and more haggard
her white hair surpassing the river in its swiftness

in order to preserve a complete memory of the years of famine
she speaks, she has never spoken
she only mutters to herself, faintly
like the voice of heaven: this isn't
a famine. this isn't
a famine.

her eyes encircle the river
encircle the broad earth

from ARIA FOR GUISHAN ISLAND

Guishan Island lies off the north-eastern coast of Taiwan

we have already fallen
into a black sea, been struck
against the land that we pursued from afar

but that other shore, on that other shore
are surging tides of humanity—another
    conflagration
is burning

oh, then I'll just lay my body down
I'll use my proud head, and imagine myself
transformed into a land of gold
letting these fin-de-siècle waves slap
my two paddle feet

Translations by Andrea Lingenfelter

Three Poems

WATER! WATER!

Mouths cracked like a turtle shell
The broad fields of my village
Shout to the ditches:
Water! Water! Give us water!

Beds parched and bare
The ditches, big and small, of my village
Shout to the reservoirs:
Water! Water! Give us water!

Burning with unconcealed anxiety
The huge mountain reservoirs
Shout to the sky:
Water! Water! Give us water!

Innocently, the overcast sky
Bitterly protests:
The rain I give every season
Has not diminished
Never have I shorted you

It is you   with your savage severing
Of the lifeblood of deep-rooted water
It is you   with your unbridled excavation
Of soil and stones that firmly hold the slopes in place
It is you   with your paving over of green fields
Who break the water cycle

I care not to imagine the following scene
The mouth of every resident of the island
Pressed close to dry faucets
Connected to empty pipes and silted reservoirs
And shouting, imploring the sky
Water! Water! Give us water!

ONE KILOMETER OF COASTLINE

Another development memo
Orders the saws to mow down
Thousands of trees, felling them one after another

The seabirds have no place to perch
They can't speak, all they can do is clamor
Circling in the darkening light of dusk

Another stretch of coastline
Instantly loses a screen
With an opening, the wind-whipped sand
Engulfs a run-down fishing village

Every sigh from my coastal
Cities and villages, set sadly adrift,
Becomes a thirsty longing
For a kilometer-long stretch of shoreline
    Windbreaks to withstand the wind and dryness

They spread dense roots to hold the sand in place
Wave green branches
Like green scarves blowing in the wind
Blocking the cold wind from the sea

O, if only a kilometer-long stretch of shoreline
Windbreaks, green and luxuriant
Can work in concert with the green mountains
To protect the environment of this lovely isle

And then, unawares, it's night again
The dim lights
Face one another and yawn
Youthful passions
Are something from a long, long time ago

And then all hollow sounds
Are suspended in
Your even blanker gaze
What can a Chopin or Debussy
Save

In the stammering passage of time
I'm but a piece of driftwood
A piece of driftwood at the water's mercy
Hastily ends another day in exhaustion
And drifting about the water, there is
Nothing good to be said about the past
Nothing remains
Save the wounds that
Await your dressing and your caress

Now at hand, now far away, you
Showed me your untellable loneliness
And asked me for support
But I'm just a piece of driftwood
A piece of driftwood at the water's mercy
In the stammering passage of time
Tossed about on one whirlpool and another
Gradually a toll is taken

Translations by John Balcom

Starting Out

The man seemed to know this place. Quan pulled the car over by a restaurant just as it got dark. I got out with the man, but he said, "Go away…" I translated. Quan said, "Ask him when we're going back." I translated. The man seemed upset. "Late." Quan waved at me. "Get in the car then. Let's go find something to eat."

Lights were coming on in the town, but the road was still dark. The old villas lit by dim neon lights slowly faded toward the back. On our right was the sea. It was big and had changed colors since the afternoon. The mountain was getting darker and darker. Quan peered ahead, his arms bent around the steering wheel, his tattoo showing prominently.

"Where's he from?" he asked, his face expressionless.

"Austria."

We stayed silent for a while. The car entered the town, shops and restaurants appearing on either side. Quan slowed the car down, his eyes darting from side to side. "Let's look for a restaurant," he said.

I eyed the ones along the right-hand side, but could not distinguish the restaurants from the cafés under the tiny lamps. The town, small and simple, suited me.

The car pulled to a stop. Quan stood in the door of a restaurant, staring at the plates of food spread out all over. I swallowed my saliva.

"What'd you want to eat?" he asked.

"Whatever," I replied. "This place looks good."

Quan squeezed his eyebrows, called out, "Mam!"

He ordered enough food to cover the table. I filled up soon. Quan stuck a spoon in the soup and stirred it. "Eat."

I wasn't used to eating slowly. Quan got busy eating again, then looked up. "Well, eat."

"You go ahead."

He smiled. "I am." He seemed to be in a better mood. "Your first job?"

"Yes, first time."

"You speak English very well."

I said nothing.

"Are you afraid?"

"Of what?"

"Oh, of speaking to a Westerner, like this one." He waved his arm.

"No."

He nodded his head. "That's good. But in general, whatever we're not good at, what we don't know—that'll make us afraid, huh?"

"You're right."

He took a toothpick and picked his teeth. I waited. He looked out on the road. "There's more for you to learn out there."

I knew that certainly. Sitting there and eating with him was different from eating ice cream with my friends. This restaurant was also far different from our usual ice-cream shop. When we'd graduated, we prepared ourselves for such differences. There wasn't anything too difficult to adjust to.

"I know, I'll get used to it," I said.

"Yes."

The woman selling food was making noises as she cleared the dishes.

"Why didn't he ask you to eat with him?" Quan asked suddenly.

"I don't know. I only translate."

He shook his head. "Strange!"

I said nothing.

He stretched his legs, turned his chest so that his bones cracked. "Mam. The bill…"

I fidgeted.

"Let me," he said.

It was dark now. We went to the beach. The chairs and umbrellas had been folded up and arranged into dark masses. The deserted beach made me feel lonely. During the day, this place would be busy, but at night there was nothing left but the paltry shops without light. It was sad.

I'd been here before. The last time was with some friends. It was summer, and we walked along the beach, the girls barefoot and kicking up the white foam. Up above, the lighthouse swept rays of light out to the sea. I'd been up there, too. Up in the lighthouse, the wind blew hard like a storm. I'd grabbed hold of the railings made of small iron bars, and my girlfriend had, too. I held on to her hand, turned to the sea, and felt that we were at the highest point people could get to. But I was also terrified, fearing that the wind would blow us away like birds.

Quan tapped me on the shoulder. "What time is it?"

I covered the watch, guessing at the positions of the glowing dots. "Ten o'clock."

"Is it time to go get that guy?"

I nodded.

He drove along the road with the long wall of rock on one side. There were many people who had come out to look at the sea. They were all lovers. I glanced through my window. They were hugging each other. On one side was the mountain, on the other the sea, and up above, the wind blew hard. They were all lovers, they were all one. I tugged at my coat. It was cold.

"Did you have fun in school?" He turned to me.

"Oh, yes." I was kind of surprised.

"How come my younger one complained?"

"There are things that aren't fun."

He shook his head. "You guys are such kids."

I turned hot. His sibling must be some sissy prince, or a timid girl. I always find a way to manage for myself; I always know the best way to adapt. I always believe I know how to change color to match the colors in life. I believe I will succeed.

Quan sat as still as a statue. Only his hands were moving on the steering wheel.

Here and there on the street, lights were coming from the oil lamps that looked like miniature lighthouses. There were cigarette cabinets. The sellers were young girls with garish makeup. I knew what they really were. One lifted her skirt, stretching out her milky legs in front of our car light. Quan honked his horn, and she withdrew her legs. Through the car window, I saw her covering her mouth to smile. We continued on.

The restaurant appeared under the pleasing light—a small place.

We squeezed through the door. It was bright inside. A girl approached us. "Brother…"

Quan turned around. "Miss, where's the Westerner?"

"Asleep." The girl smiled.

"A room upstairs?" Quan asked.

"Yes."

Quan looked at me. "Well?"

"Let him sleep," I said.

The girl came closer, raising her hands to tie up her hair, showing a white belly. Her round face looked fresh, and she rubbed herself up against Quan.

"Why don't you stay here for the night, brother?"

Quan calmly put an arm on the girl's shoulder, his other hand going inside her shirt. I turned away.

"You're very cute. Another time."

The girl was unruffled. "Liar!"

Quan waved to me. "Let's go."

The girl walked out the door. The light from the restaurant showed off her sexy body. Quan revved the engine.

I kept thinking about the girl, feeling really warm. Quan drove to a sandbar. I left the car. It was windy. I held on to the door, feeling like I was being lifted up. I remembered the girl's full breasts on his arm; I remembered his forceful hand under her shirt—and his air of confidence, of disdain. That's life.

I opened the car door, climbed back in. "Where are we going to sleep?"

"I'm out of money." He placed his chin on his arm and looked out to the sea.

I looked at him. Taking in a deep breath, I said, "Let's go back there."

"Where?"

"That place. I brought some money—there's plenty…" I looked away.

Silence. I felt awkward. "Well?"

He looked sideways at me, twisted his lips. "No."

I felt chilly all of a sudden. He took out a cigarette, lit it. He stayed pensive. I sat still.

It must have been really late. He drove slowly toward the road, then pulled the car over to a spot where there was no wind. He went out to block the tire, then came back inside. "You sleep in the back."

I climbed to the back. "What about you?"

"Don't mind me," he said softly.

I laid myself down, bending my arms to make a pillow. The seat cushions were soft. I closed my eyes. For nearly twenty years, I'd only known school, but I was an adult now, a mature person. Twenty years—not a short amount of time in a life. I was earning money on my own. I wasn't afraid of anything. Absolutely nothing. But why was he showing me such disdain? Wasn't he interested in such things? I didn't understand.

Quan took a drag from his cigarette, then flipped it away. He must have heard me moving. He reached over the front seat to place a hand on my shoulder. I put my face to the back of the seat. I sensed him smiling.

"Go to sleep."

I pretended not to hear. I suddenly missed home, missed my desk. Missed the yellow lamp I had on the desk, as well as the window facing my neighbor's house. Yes, I needed to go to sleep. Tomorrow I'd confuse the experience with a dream and then I'd be calm enough to start out all over again.

Then I calmly went to sleep for what was left of the night.

Translation by Nguyen Qui Duc

Thuong

When Miss Thuong first arrived, Mr. Hao was outside gardening. Out of breath, she dropped her suitcase in the yard, unbuttoned her collar, and blew inside her blouse to cool herself off.

Hao was so flustered that he threw down his spade near the bed of roses, wiped his hands on his trousers, and muttered, "Oh dear me—very good, very good. Come in, come in!"

Even though the difference in their ages was great, they were good friends. He hadn't seen her for about three years, and except for being a little heavier, she hadn't changed a bit. The corners of her eyes were sharp as knives, her mouth wide, and her lips a deep red. She had long legs and strode on them as gracefully as a leopard.

Hao asked her why she had come to his remote town. She smiled.

"Oh, I felt sad and decided I needed to take a trip. As for why this town, well, it was actually at the suggestion of a friend. She said that if I was feeling sad, I should go far away. And this place has both mountains and sea. And when I was on the bus, I suddenly remembered an old acquaintance I had here. Luckily, I'd written down the address in my book."

Hao had been busy brewing *nhan tran* tea, but on hearing those words, the heightened sense of anticipation he'd felt since she arrived died. He knew his disappointment was his own fault, though. He kept up an animated façade, and they both chattered enthusiastically. Thuong had her own style of telling stories. Each new piece of information was followed by a few sharp commentaries, all sarcastic. But her remarks were not meant to be malicious—unlike those of his wife, now dead, who used to make jibes during festive occasions and the Tet holiday that were always a source of discomfort for him.

Thuong liked to smile, and when she did, her eyes sparkled like water in a spring, often startling people. Suddenly, she stopped in the middle of a sentence, turned around, and asked with whom he was staying. He pretended to smile sadly.

"Nobody."

It was true; he lived alone in this house, which his children had repaired for him the previous year. When he had requested that they paint all of his blinds green, they had called him trendy. Now, for the first time in his life, he had a guest room, though he had yet to have a guest. He asked Thuong if she would mind staying in his house. She laughed and said her reputation wouldn't suffer; she had been running around for some time and was no longer a naive girl.

This statement stirred up some hope in Hao, and his enthusiasm quickly returned. He took a small desk fan from the cupboard—the same fan that would leap like a toad onto his bed in the morning, after it had been on all night. He gave Thuong a pink, Thai-made fan and saved the defective one for himself. Then he mopped the guest room and unrolled a floral mat on the bed.

Finished, he stood back to take in the whole picture, his eyes wide as a child's.

"Anything missing?" he asked Thuong.

She was all smiles.

"It's just fine, Uncle. First rate."

Thuong stayed away from the house all day. When she returned, she washed her clothes and sang melodious Russian songs. She looked absent-minded, like a person being rocked gently back and forth in an ox-drawn cart. The pace of life in this place had awakened in her a strange feeling of purity. She would go into the garden, knife in hand, and return with a few nameless flowers and sheaves of withered grass, just enough to fill a vase and make Hao blush at this reminder of how countrified and monotonous his life was.

And she cooked. Mostly simple food, but when she had more time, she'd rustle up sophisticated dishes.

On one holiday, Hao's grandson Lam, a student who lived in the city, came for a visit during his summer break. Stretched out on the hammock, he said spontaneously, "If only I had a braised duck!" Thuong didn't say a word, but smiled to herself.

That evening, the two men feasted on braised duck washed down with apricot wine. Picking the lotus seeds from the duck's belly, Lam asked, "Does Thuong run a restaurant?" He waited for her to come home so that he could congratulate her. But she didn't come back. Finally, at ten, Hao urged him to go home so that his parents wouldn't worry.

The road was steep and long, but Hao was insistent that the young man—the only member of his family who had made it to university—leave and get his sleep. Seeing him to the garden gate and feigning indifference, Hao said, "It's certain she will not be back tonight."

Lam smiled. "The lady seems to be untamed."

He started his motorbike. Hao watched its red rear light zigzag down the hill and disappear into the darkness.

Two days later, when Lam came back, his grandfather was ill. Lam found him sitting in the middle of the house, wrapped in a red blanket as if he were about to hold a séance. He spoke through a stuffed-up nose.

"Is that you, Lam? I'm going to have a steam bath."

Then he sneezed repeatedly.

Thuong emerged from the kitchen, her eyes shining, her complexion ruddy. She smiled. "Be careful—I don't want you to stick your foot into this pot of water. Go in first, and I'll bring it in after you."

Lam, who had stretched out his legs on the divan and was reading a newspaper, hurriedly lowered his feet, greeted her, and then returned to his reading. All of a sudden, something prompted him to look up. Thuong was bending over, stretching her long arms down to pick up the pot of steaming water. Silhouetted through her thin clothes, her body looked as beautiful and pure as an ancient statue, though she had a look of resignation on her face. Lam jumped up. "Let me take that for you," he said. And then he asked himself, *Why do I suddenly feel so noble and manly?*

Thuong handed him two pieces of cloth, her gesture confident rather than shy. Lam searched for something to say.

"Where did you get the leaves for the steam bath?"

"From the garden," Thuong said softly, walking behind him.

Lam pictured her carrying the basket, her hair unkempt, pictured her hands picking the leaves.

"I feel ill also," he said. "Do you think I need a steam bath?"

Three days elapsed, but Thuong hadn't returned. Hao had ventured into her room and found that everything was just as she'd left it before saying she was going to the market to buy a few things. He lay on the cot, and then he sat on the divan. He skimmed through the newspapers, but didn't take in a thing.

Late in the morning, as he was napping, he heard the noise of motorbikes at the gate. He didn't rise. He was angry with her. She was so impulsive. At times she was hardworking and considerate, a kind-hearted housewife; at other times, she could behave like a whore. Now some people had come for her, probably the artists she'd been looking for.

"Daddy! Daddy!" His daughter's piercing voice sounded like a policewoman's—even more authoritative than usual.

He heard Lam's voice also: "Hao, my parents are here."

Lam walked in, went into the kitchen, stayed there for a while, and then came out, saying nothing.

Ngoc, Hao's daughter, asked solemnly, "Are you all right now?" She glanced surreptitiously at her husband, as if signaling him to do something they had planned. "We'll stay for lunch with Daddy, right?"

The noises Ngoc made from the kitchen—the meat being cut, the water being poured over vegetables—would not allow Hao to forget Thuong.

She would often wear a sleeveless dress of thin, printed cotton and would sing, the sun shining on her, as she drew water from the well. In the evening, she stretched out her legs on the floor and cooked dinner by the fire. Whenever he pictured this scene, it was as if the two of them were lost in a deep cavern, out of earshot of all other human voices. Only the sound of a falling coconut frond could bring him back to reality…

Nobody, including Lam, mentioned Thuong.

Only two days before, he and Lam had laughed together. His grandson had stayed with him until midnight and at the gate had asked, "Thuong often goes for walks, doesn't she?"

Now, it wasn't until the round tray had been placed on the table that Ngoc asked with a smile, "Daddy, where is Thuong?"

"How should I know?" Hao replied.

Ngoc concentrated on sorting the chopsticks into pairs. "Then when will she leave?"

"I don't know."

His son-in-law put down the newspaper and said proprietarily, "Let's eat."

They all sat at the table. But the atmosphere was heavy and not at all like the other days when his children would come to visit. "We want to say something, Daddy," Ngoc began, but she was interrupted by the sudden appearance of Thuong in the doorway.

She looked even more beautiful and careless than usual. With her quiet, leopard's grace, she made a slight bow.

"Good morning, everyone."

Hao pointed. "This is my daughter, and my son-in-law. And this is Thuong."

Thuong smiled again, looking at Phuong, the son-in-law. "Yes. How do you do?"

"Will you join us for lunch?" Hao asked.

Thuong shook her head. "No, thank you. All of you, please go ahead; I've eaten already."

She passed behind the table, her handbag brushing gently against Phuong's chair. Phuong thought, *She hasn't changed.*

Hao felt relieved. His anger vanished.

He heard the sound of water being drawn from the well. "Have a rest before you take a bath," he called to Thuong, starting to rise out of his chair. "You don't want to catch a cold."

"I'll go!" Lam said quickly, then jumped up.

He went into the kitchen, opened a jar, and extracted a few hot chilies. When he got out to the well, he saw that Thuong was shampooing her long, black hair, revealing the nape of her snow-white neck. He completely forgot what he'd wanted to say, blushed, and went back into the house.

Hao slept. The old man's mouth opened and closed as he breathed in and out. Ngoc lay curled on the divan like a homeless person on a sidewalk. Looking at her, Phuong was suddenly struck by the thought that his wife was terribly ugly and looking more and more like her mother. And she was too talkative and told the same, bland jokes. And just like her mother, she went on and on, day after day, year after year, as monotonous as a clock.

Phuong rose and walked over to the closed door of the inner room, lingering there. Perhaps Thuong was sleeping, her black hair spread all over the pillow. He remembered the way she would lie, peacefully, as if in a meadow, breathing so lightly. Sometimes, at night, he would shake her gently, to see if she was still alive. Those days were so distant now. But she seemed exactly the same. He knew she was easy; he knew he was a man who didn't mind taking advantage of her Western ways. He'd thought their relationship was a good one. But it turned out he was just another of her distractions. The way she had left had offended him. She had been completely indifferent, as if he were a whore whom she was fed up with and was simply abandoning. The only thing that had comforted him that day was the knowledge that he had deceived her; to the very last minute, she had thought he was unmarried. He had been lying. But then again, he wondered if knowing his marital status would have had any real effect on that woman, that tramp.

All these thoughts passed through Phuong's head as he stood by her door. He raised his hand to knock, but at that moment the door opened and she came out. She gave him a wry smile. "Well, well, aren't you bold? But you'd better get out of here quickly—your wife is up already."

Instinctively, Phuong spun around. Then, feeling ridiculous, he turned to her and frowned. "What are you doing here?"

Thuong stood in the doorway, her arms akimbo, her hair tangled. "You can be sure that it wasn't to look for you."

Ngoc could be heard coughing.

"I'm sorry to have lied to you," Phuong said hastily. "At the time, my wife and I—"

Thuong waved his words away. "It doesn't matter to me—what difference does it make?" Then, as if by impulse, she burst out laughing. Taken aback, Phuong raised his hand as if he was going to cover her mouth. Instead, he spun around and walked quickly into the garden, kicking dead coconuts out of his path as he went.

The commotion woke the whole house. Lam, who had been picking berries from some wild bushes in the back, rushed in to see what the laughter was all about. At the kitchen door, he caught sight of Thuong putting her hair up in a bun, her eyes shining. She waved to him and said, "If someone asks, just say I was laughing with you." Lam nodded. At that moment, his mother walked in, a concerned expression on her face. "I'm sorry," Thuong said softly, lowering her head.

"It's my fault," Lam interjected. "I was joking."

"Get in!" Ngoc shouted at him, and short mother and tall son went back into the main room of the house.

That afternoon, Thuong left, carrying the same large suitcase and wearing the same clothes as on the day she'd arrived. Hao looked older. He insisted to her that this was his house and that she could stay as long as she wanted and that Ngoc had no right...

Thuong smiled. "I'm just leaving because it's been a long trip—nothing more, Uncle."

"Let me see her as far as the bus station," said Lam. He insisted on strapping the suitcase to the front of his motorbike so that he could be closer to her. He started the bike, and off they went. Below was the vast, indifferent sea. Thuong gazed at the nape of young Lam's neck. How many years had it been since she'd last been stirred this way? She felt she was about to embark on another adventure, another game of hide and seek. After some hesitation, some struggle with herself, she said, "You know, I don't want to go straight home. Take me to the Hong Hoa Hotel. Tomorrow afternoon, if you have some time, meet me and take me to the beach."

"What time?" Lam said.

When he arrived the next day exactly at five o'clock, the people at the hotel told him she had just left. First she had given them a letter, they said, but then she had taken it back. If he went after her quickly enough, they said, he might still be able to catch her.

Translation by Nam Son and Wayne Karlin

Three Stories

BENEATH THE BLOSSOMS

Late at night, around the time the dog, husband, and children were sleeping peacefully, Keiko touched up her makeup, getting ready to meet someone. She told no one about this, not because she needed to keep it a secret, but because there was no need to tell others. There was another world and she had been seeing people from that world, and it would be difficult for anyone to understand such an explanation.

Keiko looked at her reflection in the mirror. Because she had applied her evening makeup, her face emitted a bewitching phosphorescence that seemed to confirm her transportation to the other world. When she felt the presence of someone outside, she got up and slipped out of the house. She passed through the walls and doors at will.

When she went out into the garden, Mr. Satō was standing outside bathed in moonlight. "Sorry to keep you waiting," she said. Mr. Satō returned her commonplace greeting, and she realized that he was walking without drawing a shadow behind him. *Pretty amazing*, she thought. She also cast no shadow at that time. Along the way, she patted the head of a dog, but it gave no sign of awakening. This was a ritual—a sign that she had been transported to the other world.

Long ago, they had made a pledge to go cherry-blossom viewing at night. Even in Keiko's garden, there was a cherry tree in full bloom. Because it was a Somei Yoshino variety of cherry tree, the blossoms floated in their eerie whiteness like clouds against the night sky. "This is the kind of cherry blossom that drives people mad," said Mr. Satō. Keiko quite agreed. Without doubt, if you spent a night under the blossoms and a full moon, the combined effect of the spirits of the moonlight and blossoms would drive you crazy.

"In the past, it was probably mountain cherries," said Keiko as she imagined the cherry that appeared around the rustic cottage in Sagano in the Nō play *Saigyō's Cherry Blossoms*. This thought was somehow transmitted to Mr. Satō, who said, "We could go there if you'd like." Smiling, he took her hand, and they easily traversed both time and space. The two of them appeared in the garden of the cottage.

While Keiko was talking, she recalled again that Mr. Satō was Saigyō. Despite this, she thought that neither Saigyō nor Satō Norikiyo suited him. The Mr. Satō who sometimes visited Keiko's place or whom she saw in town was a person with a handsome face and a tall, lean figure. He wore stylish tweed jackets and was a gentleman of no discernible occupation. Even though he was clearly older than Keiko, it was hard to determine his age. He looked as if he had lived an awfully long time without looking aged—especially his beautiful hands, which seemed to defy both age and gender. They possessed an elegance that could only have been acquired by having lived and played hundreds of years with blossoms, moon, and snow.

Holding Keiko's hand, Mr. Satō said, "How do you like these cherry blossoms?"

"These are the mountain cherries Saigyō liked so much," said Keiko, covering Mr. Satō's hand with her other one. She was a little embarrassed that she had mentioned Saigyō's name. "He probably liked cherries such as these, which have blossoms and leaves mixed together, don't you think?"

Just like she said, the old cherry tree spread forth branches laden with countless delicate blossoms and leaves like a figure wearing a canopy, shimmering in a haze of strange gentleness and splendor superimposed on the figure of Mr. Satō. No, it was the venerable priest Saigyō. Mr. Satō muttered this passage from *Saigyō's Cherry Blossoms*:

anshitsu no hana wa	Blossoms at the hermitage,
hana ippon	only one tree
waga hitori	for me alone—
nagamuru mono mo	I had thought there would be
waga to hana to yori	no one other than myself
hoka ni wa nashi to	who would gaze at the blossoms—
omohishi ni	just myself and my blossoms.

"First, if I were to find myself beneath the blossoms with a beautiful woman…"

"I have some *sake* here," said Keiko as she poured wine into the light-crimson ceremonial cup in Mr. Satō's hand. As he drank the wine, he gazed into her eyes. He returned the cup to her. His were not the eyes of an ordinary person. When he gazed at her, her body turned to liquid and she was overwhelmed by a mixture of sweet rapture and fear of being swallowed up like wine.

"Tonight your face looks flushed, like a blossom in bloom. Why was it that you coldly turned me away when I asked for lodging one rainy night?"

"It was because you thought I was a prostitute or some such person."

"Yes, I said that was really strange."

"Even after Saigyō renounced the world, it seems he couldn't conquer his desire for women. That's why it was written in the *Genpei Jōsuiki* [chronicles of the rise and fall of the Minamoto and Taira families] that love was actually the incentive behind renouncing the world."

"That wasn't it. It was really quite simple. I quit serving at court and thought I'd like to live just as I pleased. In any event, the world became terribly chaotic after that. I'm not bragging, but I have the ability to see the future."

"Wouldn't you say it was unlucky being secluded from the world?"

"You certainly used a difficult word. Let's just say that I was fond of material things. Fortunately, I had plenty of material resources, was secluded in nature with poetry, and had beautiful women to keep me company throughout my days."

"That's enviable."

"It seems there were many people who felt that way in those days. For example, there was a woman who followed my example and walked east and west throughout the country."

"You're talking about a person called Nijō, who wrote *Towazugatari* [the confessions of Lady Nijō]."

"Yes, the daughter of Koga Masatada, also a great beauty."

"You've met her then?"

"Of course. But it was after she died and came over to this side. I could introduce you to her next time."

Fascinated, Keiko gazed at the setting moon with eyes that were drunk from both wine and blossoms. "I think I'd like to fall asleep beneath these blossoms."

"I was just thinking that myself," said Mr. Satō.

"I wonder what would happen if we were to fall asleep. It seems like we would die, our spirits drained by the blossoms in full bloom."

"Shall we try?"

Mr. Satō now took the form of the priest Saigyō. Keiko thought in a corner of her mind that as long as she was going to die, she'd like to do so just like Saigyō—beneath the blossoms, as he had predicted in his poem:

negawaku wa	Would that I could
hana no shita nite	beneath the blossoms
haru shinamu	die in spring
so no kisaragi no	around the second month
mochizuki no koro	under a full moon.

"It happened just as you said in your poem, didn't it? How were you able to do it? It seems like you just stopped breathing."

"Yes, it was easy. Like you said, I just fell asleep under the cherry tree."

Keiko was pressed to Saigyō's chest as she listened to that voice. It was a chest that couldn't be thought human. "Who are you? The spirit of the cherry?" she tried to say, but she couldn't utter those words. She heard the sound of his voice in her body. They melted together and could not be distinguished one from the other. Keiko felt that she had been swallowed up and was locked inside the black trunk of a ghost tree. Not knowing whether it was her body, her soul, or both that had been sucked into the tree, she felt herself melting into the sap of the cherry tree. Or had she become the sap itself? She sensed herself becoming a clear green liquid. She thought that the pleasant voices she heard were the numerous spirits talking to each other. When she thought of asking Mr. Satō about this, a voice replied that it was so.

"This is where spirits that have been sucked into the cherry tree gather to chat and exchange pledges of love."

"Like us," said Keiko joyfully.

The long-lasting rapture had an attractive plantlike nature that turned this and that into a green sap and had no connection to the animal-like fury of the flesh. With the flow of time, the rapture deepened, the cherry blossoms scattered ceaselessly, like the quiet joy that made bodies tremble.

She couldn't remember whether Mr. Satō had sent her there or they had parted somewhere along the way, but she was fast asleep in her room when she was awakened by the sound of her dog and child. Outside the window, she sensed an overwhelming spring light, and the garden looked like a jewelry box turned upside down.

"Mom, the cherry tree's split open."

When Keiko went out into the garden, the line "the sound of the wind and rain arriving at night" came to mind when she saw a surprisingly thick bed of fallen blossoms scattered around the old cherry tree.

Keiko's daughter said, "It looks like it's bleeding green blood." From the trunk of the old, cruelly rent tree, green sap came flowing as if it were indeed blood, staining blossoms and making tiny bubbles as it was sucked into the black earth. Keiko wondered if this was the result of last night's pleasure and if this tree was actually the cherry tree belonging to the priest Saigyō in Sagano.

She thought, *This is scary,* but instead she said, "Last night's rain and wind were quite severe." She put her palms together for the sake of the dead cherry.

Before anyone noticed it, the dog wagged his tail and lapped up the flowing sap. When the child shouted, "Stop that!" the dog looked surprised and turned to face her. Then he turned around, scratched his head with a hind leg, and let out a long yawn. On a Sunday morning like this, it was hard to discuss in detail what had occurred during the night. Keiko followed the dog's example and yawned.

When the young girl first appeared, Keiko felt as if one of her daughter's classmates had called out her name. She had suddenly stepped into another world, and for a second her mind had trouble adjusting. In any case, the young girl was licking an ice-cream cone—something too early for the end of spring—and was sitting on a bench on a bright avenue, beneath a cherry tree that had just shed its blossoms and was bursting forth with fresh, young leaves tinged with red. Before Keiko could ask who she was, the young girl explained, "I'm Nijō. I believe Mr. Satō told you about me." It was then Keiko realized that what had happened the other night beneath the blossoms was being continued in the middle of the city in broad daylight.

"Oh, you're the Nijō of *Towazugatari*," Keiko said to verify. The young girl showed her the cover of a book she was holding and laughed. It was an annotated version of *Towazugatari*. Her mannerisms, appearance, and hairstyle were those of a female junior-college student who had chosen *Towazugatari* as the topic of a graduation thesis. But Keiko never for a moment doubted that this young girl had come to her from that other world. Her face, lit by the sun shining between the leaves of the tree, showed a strange transparency, which indicated that she was not a person of this world even though she looked like a beautiful girl who seemed oppressed by the chaos of city life. It seemed as if her flesh had dissolved from some deep sorrow, making her look transparent. Outwardly, she was a persistently cheerful young girl, but the proposal she came to consult Keiko about seemed ridiculous coming from such a person.

"Actually, there's something I need you to help me with," said Nijō as she looked up at Keiko, her eyes sparkling. "I want to get even with Papa. Using *kayuzue* as a pretext, Papa had some senior male nobles beat female courtiers like me half in jest. This time, I want to capture Papa and give him a sound beating."

"What is *kayuzue*?"

"Oh, that's when kindling wood that had been used to stir the fire to make *azuki*-bean gruel was used to hit women on their bottoms to encourage the birth of male offspring. But wouldn't it be stupid if only male children were born?"

"That may well be, but when you say 'Papa,' are you referring to the retired sovereign Go-Fukakusa? I wonder if it is all right to exact revenge on such a person."

"Sure it is, because Papa is a little masochistic," asserted the girl, her face flushed.

"Then would you go out in broad daylight to perform things like a beating?"

"Anytime is all right, but I'll come by to get you at nighttime."

Keiko considered Nijō's plot. She returned home and reread relevant sections of *Towazugatari*. After Nijō and Higashi no Onkata conspired and "hit the retired sovereign as hard as they wanted," he was on the verge of getting seriously angry. Keiko was feeling a little uncomfortable about assisting in things that could produce complications later, but her curiosity moved her to join in the amusements and pranks of the nobility.

Fourteen years older than Nijō, the retired sovereign had been initiated as a youth into the ways of love by Nijō's mother, Dainagon no Suke. Thereafter, he considered Nijō to be his possession from the time she was still in her mother's womb, waiting to be born, until he finally possessed her when she was fourteen years old. This part made Keiko think of Genji initiating Murasaki no Ue in amours. Nijō was sixteen when she bore the retired sovereign a child. Keiko was able to understand that Nijō called her lover "Papa" because he was a father figure to her.

That night while it was raining, she sensed someone tapping on the window from the garden side. When she went outside, it was the other world without either rain or darkness, and Nijō was standing there dressed like a female courtier in ancient scroll paintings.

"I've just escorted His Majesty to a place nearby," said Nijō. Now she called the sovereign "His Majesty" instead of "Papa."

Keiko saw a building in the Azumaya style further off in the garden. No such structure should have been there, so her head was in a state of confusion. But Nijō led her by the hand to the building, where she found a corridor connected to it. In no time at all, Keiko found herself inside a dark room. Fragrant incense filled the air. She thought that the strange antique light that filled the room emanated from small offering tables surrounding the gilded folding screen.

"When His Majesty comes in, please restrain his arms."

"I don't possess superhuman strength."

"That's all right. Papa is a small, weak, childlike man," said Nijō, reverting back to modern expression. A person wrapped in a flowerlike robe appeared unexpectedly. *That's all there is to him,* Keiko thought. As if in a daze, she mounted a frontal attack on him. Strangely enough, she encountered no resistance. Time and time again, she felt as if she had put her arms around stiff robes inflated with air. Soon she realized that she herself was wrapped in similar robes, unable to move about freely.

Even though it seemed that men of those days were of exceedingly small stature, she gathered her strength. Nijō circled behind the retired sovereign, lifted up his robes, and seemed to be beating him on the buttocks with a slender branch. He let out a sharp sound and screamed. It was a sweet-sounding scream, quite inconceivable for a man over the age of thirty.

"Please don't beat me so hard," the retired sovereign said in a sobbing voice. "I won't have the buttocks of female courtiers beaten anymore, so please forgive me." But Nijō continued beating him mercilessly. Just as

Keiko was about to tell her that was enough and she should forgive him, Keiko was pushed and fell face up.

Right before her eyes, an oval face that looked like a Girl's Day doll closed in on her. That the face was not masculine or rough was uncanny. Moreover, it was as small as a Nō mask. For some reason, she was not able to move around. Both she and the sovereign were wrapped in something like large flower petals and were robbed of freedom of movement. A flowerlike fragrance and a faint gold light filled the air, and Keiko knew she had come to a place not of this world.

She tried to say, "Nijō, what in the world is happening?" but she couldn't speak. She was wrapped in the embrace of someone who seemed to be the sovereign. Perhaps it would be better to say that she felt as if she had become an insect and was trapped inside a blossom room. If she was a butterfly, then it seemed the sovereign was a sharp stamen coming to meet the butterfly inside the blossom, and that thought made Keiko feel as if he were a real man.

"When I first saw you, I thought you were like a cherry blossom, if I were to use the metaphor of flowers. When you hid your face in your sleeve, it was like cherry blossoms cloaked in haze. I was teased by that child who knew I had to have my way with you, so I had her summon you here," he whispered. While he was doing so, Keiko's body felt numb, as if it were inside clouds or haze.

"Even if you say things like that now, I know that later on you and Nijō will lie in bed chatting about how 'the cherry blossom's color was beautiful, but its branch was brittle and broke too easily' or some such nonsense."

"I don't want you to worry about Nijō. She will just stay there and burn with jealousy about the two of us being together, but she must see the whole story to the end as punishment for beating me a little while ago."

While this voice teased Keiko's ears, she felt herself becoming a large blossom and the sovereign gradually shrinking until he was as small as Issunbōshi [Little One Inch]. She felt him diving into the blossom's crowded center. As if she were injected by a sweet, poisonous liquid, her body and consciousness became paralyzed and intoxication rippled through her. A blossom, her body opened rather unbecomingly as if to the four directions.

She heard the faraway voice of the sovereign, drenched in tears, saying, "How am I to awaken from this unexpected dream of a night that could only have occurred in another world?" She slipped out of the blossom room, or would it be better to say that she felt herself evaporating and dispersing like the fragrance of a flower?

When she awakened, it was a rainy morning, but though her mind was still numb, there was no mistaking she had returned to this world. She was surprised by a light tapping sound at her window. When she looked, she saw peering at her a young girl whose face was shaded blue from standing under a hydrangea-colored umbrella.

"Sorry about last night," Nijō said in a voice that sounded a little depressed. "Papa asked me to deliver a 'morning-after poem,' but I don't have the letter."

Keiko thought that Nijō had probably thrown away the letter on the way over. Though Keiko was the one who should have been consoled, she reconsidered when she saw how remorseful Nijō looked. "Don't worry about it. It seems I'm the one who ought to thank you."

"No, not at all," said the young girl with a sad-looking smile. "Papa is a strange person. He likes to make love to other women in front of me like he did with you, and he drives me away from him to make love to other men. Sometimes I think that, despite being small and weak, he may be a kind of goblin."

Then the young girl told pointless stories before leaving. At some point, Keiko remembered that Nijō had said she would like to become like Mr. Satō—that is, like Saigyō. That feeling was born when Nijō was around nine years old, and she said that it was intensifying. Nijō had renounced the world when she was past thirty and had embarked on a journey inconceivable for a woman of that time, travelling from Kamakura in the east to Ashizuri in the west.

About two months later, it was decided that Keiko would travel to Europe. When she was boarding a plane for the flight overseas, she noticed a woman over thirty sitting to the left in her row. It was a face she had seen somewhere before. The black dress somehow looked like a nun's habit. In an instant, Keiko realized that the woman was Nijō. Nijō raised her hand slightly and smiled. After Keiko waved in return, she closed her eyes. While she was absorbed in thoughts about Nijō traveling to foreign countries to seek paramours, she drifted off to sleep.

CASTLE IN THE SEA

Crossing the sky borne on the first winds of summer, Keiko was flying over the English Channel. After finishing some business in Milan and Paris, she was heading to Penzance, a harbor town on the tip of the Cornwall peninsula, to see an eccentric English writer who lived there. It was the final destination of her trip.

At some point when she felt the not-very-large plane draw close to the surface of the sea, she looked out the window and saw something that looked like a castle reflected in the water under the bright, clear sky. She saw towers and ramparts, even a forest. She thought that this might be a mirage seen from the sky, but usually mirages were seen at water level. She had never heard of mirages in the sea visible from the sky. She thought that perhaps it was the other world imposing itself on her consciousness again. While she was thinking of the dead people who lived in that world, suddenly the names of King Mark of Cornwall, Tristan, and Isolde floated into her mind. She started to try to traverse the stage on which the tale of Tristan and Isolde unfolded.

Tristan, nephew of King Mark of Cornwall, had gone to Ireland to seek Isolde of the golden locks. As Tristan was taking Isolde on a ship to be the king's consort, the two mistakenly drank an aphrodisiac or love potion. This had been concocted by Isolde's mother to ensure harmony in the relationship between her daughter and the King of Cornwall. Unfortunately, after they had drunk the potion, Tristan and Isolde were at once bound by a consuming love. It was as if the two had gulped down death. Isolde became Tristan's lover as she was being taken to King Mark, and events moved toward tragedy, with the two dying in the end.

Keiko was thinking about the tale compiled by Bede that she had read in her youth. Unconsciously, a suspicion floated into her mind that perhaps Isolde had intentionally made Tristan drink the potion. Tristan was a cold-hearted knight who thought nothing of handing Isolde over to King Mark. Tristan thought her neither beautiful nor desirable, even after she had nursed him back to health when he sustained injuries fighting a dragon. Since her love for him had not been returned, there seemed to be nothing else the high-ranking Isolde could do but make Tristan drink the aphrodisiac that would "bind them in death."

While Keiko was thinking about the tale, the castle in the sea disappeared. Ms. Sone, Keiko's private secretary, was sitting in the next seat and asked, "Did you see something unusual?" Keiko replied nonchalantly, "I saw the castle of the Dragon King."

In Plymouth, she prepared for bed early that night in a hotel room with a view of the sea. Her nerves were somewhat agitated since seeing the castle in the sea, so all the stone buildings lining the harbor town looked like a mirage between the deep-blue sea and the faintly bright sky.

Keiko heard someone knocking at the door. It was inconceivable that Ms. Sone would suddenly come to her room. She heard the person outside the door announce in a female voice, "It's Nijō." When she hurriedly opened the door, she found an elegant woman who looked like a nun wearing a gown. She concluded that it was the same Nijō of *Towazugatari*, who had invited her to join in the beating of the retired sovereign Go-Fukakusa during the *kayuzue* incident of the other day. Just a few days ago, Nijō had been a young girl of about fourteen, but now she was a woman past thirty. Keiko thought that the flow of time in that other world must differ from ours.

"When we left Japan, I thought I saw you on the plane, but this is certainly a chance meeting—seeing you in a place like this."

"I saw you in the lobby a little while ago," said Nijō. "Coincidentally, I am also going to the town at the tip of this peninsula."

"You mean Penzance?" Keiko thought about asking what sort of business Nijō had there, but stopped herself.

"From there, I'm boarding a ship to cross over to the small islands beyond the point."

"I believe they're called the Scilly Isles. Are you really going to Land's End?" Keiko thought that, from that point on, there was only the sea and beyond it nothing at all. Was Nijō planning to cross over to Ireland or something? Keiko thought that Tristan had gone to Ireland and there found Isolde of the golden locks. The two women passed the time talking and drinking handmade local mead, then Nijō stood up and said, "Wouldn't you like to come over to my room? There's an interesting view. And I also want to give you some quaint medicinal wine."

Following Nijō's suggestion, Keiko was led in a dreamlike state down the corridor of the hotel until she stood in front of an old door. When Nijō opened it, the room was filled with water as if it were the sea. Keiko was looking at a cross-section of the sea, but the water didn't flow out when the door was opened.

Keiko thought to herself, *So this was the plan,* but she did exactly as she was told and followed Nijō into the sea, moving as freely as if she had become a fish and breathing without any difficulty.

"Long ago, it was said that Genshin conjured up water like the great sea and surprised Jakushin, who had come to visit him in a residence called Eshin'in on Mount Hiei. Actually, I tried to do what he did."

"I've heard that story somewhere. It was water brimming over that touched just the glow of the surface. But even if you said this was water with color like the northern sea, there might be mermaids and mermen."

"Ages ago, there was a castle that sank in the sea, and that's where Tristan and Isolde are probably living. The two of them have probably become mermaid and merman by now."

Keiko walked in the wavering water. With a body that melted into the light of the water's color, she felt she was drifting. A crumbling castle appeared. It was like the castle in Western-style ghost movies that looks less ominous during the day because the ruined gates and walls can easily be traversed. When Keiko peered inside the tower, she saw two large fish standing on their tails and embracing each other. She gasped.

The upper half of the fish was a beautiful spindle shape, like a bonito, and covered by almost venomous-looking brilliant blue scales. But there remained something in the faces that reminded Keiko of human beings. As for the lower half of their bodies, she drank in the meaning of the strange statement Nijō had made earlier: "The two of them have probably become mermaid and merman by now." Tristan and Isolde had begun to transform into fish, but the lower parts of their white bodies were clearly human and bound in a mating position.

"Is this the fate of Tristan and Isolde?" Keiko exclaimed as she tried to look back at Nijō. But she couldn't see her.

She felt as if she were observing rare sea creatures in an aquarium as she gazed at their incessant mating in the wavering blue light. While the armless fish rubbed their chests and heads together clumsily, below their waists they were finely wrought, elegant human beings who continued to move in the most obscene manner. But rather than indulging in pleasure, it seemed as if they were trying to resist the gradual transformation of their bodies. When seen in this way, it was a most pitiful sight.

Keiko came back to herself when she heard a voice say, "We should probably leave shortly." She saw Nijō holding in her hand something that looked like a vial filled with fruit wine. Without a look of concern, Nijō turned her back on the fates of the two half-human, half-fish creatures and walked out of the water. Keiko chased after her. When she did, they were back in the hall.

"What did you find?"

"A *fuirutoru.* Namely, an aphrodisiac," Nijō said innocently as a smile stole across her face.

"Is this the famous aphrodisiac that Tristan and Isolde were supposed to have drunk accidentally?"

"Do you think it's something they would have drunk accidentally? Isolde purposely made Tristan drink it and then drank it herself." As Nijō was saying exactly what Keiko had been thinking, she prepared a small dose of reddish-purple liquid, pouring it into a glass.

Keiko was a little worried about what would happen to her if she were to drink it, but she brought it to her lips since she wasn't certain what it actually was—aphrodisiac or charm. Sweet and tasting of alcohol, it was definitely strong wine. There were supposed to be various medicinal plants mixed in, but there was no odor of Chinese herbal medicine, only a pleasant fragrance and an earnest, sweet flavor.

At that moment, a subtle transformation occurred. It was not the kind of transformation that made the body burn in yearning for someone; neither had it the effect of a strong-spirited drug. The body became empty—it was a transformation of the temperament that made you want to embrace someone with a similar void within—that is, it was a sensation that spread death, like a corrosion of the internal organs. It was without doubt a dangerous potion.

Nijō divided the remaining potion in half, giving Keiko her portion in another vial while saying, "It is frightfully efficacious when you make someone drink it."

Keiko instantly wondered who, but before the question came out, she decided to take the vial back as a secret souvenir. With the thought that she possessed a poison powerful enough to kill people at any time, her heart throbbed like that of a crazed murderer…

Translations by S. Yumiko Hulvey

Four Poems

THE HUNDRED-PACER SNAKE IS DEAD

The hundred-pacer snake is dead
Stuck in a transparent bottle of medicinal wine
The label on the bottle reads: *Aphrodisiac*
A teaser for the guys roaming the red-light district

The hundred-pacer snake of myth is dead too
The Paiwan people once believed its eggs were their ancestors
But today it sits in a transparent bottle
The agent now for promoting lust in the big city

When a man drinks the medicinal wine
And struts his false majesty into the red-light district
There, at the brothel door to meet him,
Is a descendant of the hundred-pacer snake:
a young Paiwan girl

TO WANDER

for my late friend Sajiyou

What does it mean to wander?
You had no idea
All you knew is that you had to leave
Hoping to find a permanent place to stay

At the tender age of thirteen
Still so innocent and unknowing
You went to work for twelve hours a day
Pawned to work as a welder in a factory

You bore the foul air and the long confinement
Not permitted to go out and with no wages
Your ID card held in the boss's safe
Once the three-year contract was fulfilled, you left

You ended up at a brick factory
Hauling bricks you made more money
Strong as a wild mountain boar
In the stifling hot factory
You earned the praise of your boss
But you had to leave
Simply because you were unwilling to take
The lowest pay for the heaviest work

You went to a construction site to carry bricks, sand, and gravel
You said you got paid by the load
Anyway, you had strength and your freedom
But who would have guessed
Three months later the foreman embezzled the payroll
No choice but to pawn your ID card at a shipping company

You never stopped wandering
You worked as a hauler, sleeping in a truck
You worked in a steel factory swinging a hammer, sleeping there too
You wandered to the vast ocean, hopped a fishing boat
Crossed the water to work in Saudi Arabia
Until a backhoe
Put an end to your wanderings
When it broke your back…
With your last breath you seemed to say
I understand. A man is forced to wander
And death is a release from worldly cares
Go, you wanderer
Wander to that unknown world
For perhaps it is a peaceful place

IF YOU'RE AN ABORIGINE

If you're an aborigine
Then wipe away your tears and blood
And like a huge burning tree
Light the road ahead

If you're an aborigine
Then sing out with your highland voice
In anger about your deep sufferings
Like desperate roaring waves

If you're an aborigine
Then set off the violence of your life
Like an explosive charge beneath the ground
Fiercely blowing open a pack of hypocrisy

If you're an aborigine
Then fear not the storm's tyranny
Stand tall like a mountain
Meeting all adverse blows

If you're an aborigine
Then when fate leaves you no way out
Do the only thing you can:
Fight with your back to the mountain

I REALLY DON'T KNOW

Sincere of heart
I awaited the Harvest Sacrifices
Though it was a bad year
I still had to pick the wild vegetables our ancestors liked to eat
As a way to welcome back their spirits

But three days after the Harvest Sacrifices
The court informed me
That I'd stolen the Forestry Bureau's property
I really don't know when the
Vegetables we have eaten for generations
Became public property protected by law

I really don't know what all this is about
When the kids ask me what the law is
And why we pick wild vegetables at the Harvest Sacrifices
My answer is:
I really don't know

Translations by John Balcom

LI JINWEN

Two Poems

VALUE

- On the face of the copper coin is Eve, on the back falls an apple

One copper coin jostles another, the sound pure
and distinct. With a wisp of morning fog I wipe away Adam's face
    and the snake pattern
And then begin to miss freedom.

Long, long ago…women were an egg-shaped fable
left behind in the mirror: on the face is Eve, Mary, or Snow White
reeling through the air, spiraling up to the summit of love where
she turns suddenly and falls for reality. The coin
steadies herself, wrenching apart gender until numbers bleed,
until hot tears bite into seventeen—and on the back is the other
    woman
deeply in love, pure and proud as a flame-cast butterfly.

You can bet with it: the front is night, the back daytime. Besides
    sincerity and courage,
the rest cannot be gambled. We are a beautiful and brave money,
    lavishing affection in a pocket
chinking our sorrow and joy, we are the dimples of two women,
    like dice
spinning in eternity…besides an inability to suppress a complete
    love, we
fear nothing. Even though the final gamble is loneliness.

We rise from the king's iron mold and complicated coinage with a
    clang
Ah, iron cells singing free and luminous

■ Those silver coins bought my black hair

Who put me under this harsh light? The silver of my entire body
    burns and clamors
A trembling magnifying glass carves out my mysterious flesh,
    deliberately
insinuating that I am a girl propagating desire in every nation

My voice is beautiful, like a group of girls like a string of silver bells
    in the wind
The topic is that limitless pocket change—in the family annals of
    history I am a comma
Not bad, being a comma; it indicates that after this pause in epic
    mythology the speech will continue:
A diary of love. We pin a silver butterfly medal
on a bare breast, and it brings us pain. We will become comrades
on the battleground of fire and ice, on our bodies like the night sky
sowing seeds and distant genes. I realized:

To travel far and betray the other's heart. Yet I firmly believe: two
    souls
squeezed together, repelled, consumed, are transformed into blood
    or mud and wrestled into a shape...
My fortune is having two worlds packed into a single wood-carved
    box, clanking
like the intimate clatter of coins sharing warmth. To purchase
black hair with silver, I'm willing! Death like blood-red spring
is the curtain falling: for added ambiguity, for prolonged missing

■ Stability, dense as pure gold

The glorious progressive tense, a vowel calling forth
the free will of human beings. Long, long ago...
In some corner of Greek mythology or *Thousand and One Nights*
    I see a gold coin
rolling towards me in the past tense, its tracks digging deep into flesh
A kind of implication, high-reigning silence and brilliance
A gold coin ruminating in the Old Testament archives
Re-interpreting the significance of woman, melting itself with winter
    sunlight
Melting into one side of a mirror or a belief. In light of the depths of
    being
I will see those flowing minerals and claims to value that were lost
in the relay of the centuries

Perhaps it's rusted, or oxidized, but my heart holds the highest
density, keeping me secure.
In a woman's form or the reflected light of flowers, I find
    intermittent shadows of a spirit
Refusing to wipe away worldly dust from the surface I forget
those feet that have traversed an ornate and sordid history
Already I've taken two faces of free love and built the first embryo.
    Long, long ago

I was gold, the colliding sound ringing like first light

THE REPORTER

You've written the entirety of youth as news but no one reads it
When you submit the draft and walk away
home in the distance darkens, but you don't worry.
Your departure has incited a chair to desk to keyboard debate
They argue like crackleware then suddenly fall silent. Ordinary
    people
continue ordinary lives, you record
a history without future

You hit the streets for interviews, legs spurring, cold wind urging
You dissect yourself with a camera, keyboard counting days
Ceaselessly you seek youth under the old tree, the
most stultifying coordinates in the islands of memory.

You use thumbtacks to tack yourself onto a political debate
Everyone can see the moonlight picking on you
Silent. When the crowd disperses
You begin to write descriptions of their fragrance
or festering travel

as news.
Alone in your body contemplating
those hot, frigid, steel or watery eyes
traveling in your body until you yourself are
by day after day of drafts issued away

Translations by Paul Manfredi

Three Poems

DUCKWEED

"More and more like the floating duckweed…"
Someone returned to the tribe this evening
Amid bamboo fences scattered over the mountain
Pondering the pains and regrets of history
Too much rice wine to drink
Makes for incoherent babbling

Mizunuo, you've lived a pretty good life
What makes you suffer so?
Your hut was completed before winter
The peach trees blossomed in the saddle of the mountain
    In the second month
Someone married a girl from a different village
Everyone is overjoyed
So what is it that worries you so?

"Three hundred years ago our ancestors
    wove fishnets and caught fish
Large sailing ships from the West appeared
    blocking out the sun
Fifty years later they shunned the farmed plains
Returning to the forests to hunt
Aside from fighting over the land
We lived in peace with each other
When the Japanese came, what was termed 'civilizing the savages'
Was in fact flogging, from the coast to the mountains
We've been like duckweed the last century…"

Someone returned to the tribe this evening
Rubbing the wound of history getting drunk
No one doubted his suffering
Perhaps he was mourning for his far-flung relatives

Perhaps he was angry at the destitution of the tribe
But not questioning justice and love
Though quietly drinking and talking
Though someone keeps leaving for distant places
Like a ripe fruit falling from the tree

YOUTH OF WUSHE

I don't recognize Tasiqisi's face
The 1920s are too remote from today
Grandma says the pink cherry blossoms flower for him
That day he abandoned his books and returned to his tribe
Led the Atayal people against the canons
They all died in battle, Grandma told me to look at
The monument at the head of the road

The monument is mottled
Covered with lichen
But it's still difficult to cover Tasiqisi's hard work
At the end of the 1970s I graduated from the teacher's college
And was stationed at the front lines, two years later
I took up chalk and taught in a school far from home
Constantly I complained about the wastewater and air pollution
And the problems with public transportation
I'm certain that if you came to the city
You'd be bad tempered too

The cherry blossoms still shimmer in winter
Tasiqisi gradually grows vague
The monument is still covered in lichen
The city performs and plunders
I still have to make a living
In the 1990s I'm still hoping to meet a nice girl and get married
Having a son would be nice
(The world's population is exploding)
Peaceful into old age, if you were I
I think you'd want the same

DOWN THE MOUNTAIN

At the station on the way to Baling Mountain
A woman squats quietly and humbly
While her children run around without worries
They all look very happy.
They are going down the mountain to shop
Using their harsh Mandarin and perhaps
Some gestures too.
It's the spring of 1985, I'm at the station
I saw farmers from the plains in the 1960s
Going to the city, often quiet and ill at ease

In the city, I never speak Atayal
I do my utmost to scrub my dark skin
I do my utmost to suppress my savage blood
And even suppress my childhood memories
I've learned to chat happily with others
Tie a bow tie and drink coffee
They softly pat my shoulders praising me
I suddenly felt weighed down
Today, many years later
At the station on Baling Mountain
Familiar as before, the sound of a woman
Her sadness, and the innocence of the children

Translations by John Balcom

Three Poems

LANGUAGE

Those imprisoned between teeth and mouth
give out ruminated flavor?
They always linger between ins and outs
and become the silence of the room,
while the eyes take footnotes.

The lines on the letter paper
can hardly outline the strides of words
whose oblique shapes
cover the real trace of steps
lest the morning light should
see through the erased footprints.

They say: ambiguity is a virtue.
I hide in ambiguity to
create ambiguity.

STREET CORNER

The lane is the leftover paper
which the sparrow pecked yesterday.
The wind caresses the greasy road.
What can be stirred
is some yesterday's headline.
Beside a deep dark braking trace
lies a broken headlight, the plastic pieces
figuratively extending to become various symptoms.
The garbage can throws out
domestic culture to cover the ground.
A skinny black cat
smells around awhile and walks away.

A nearly hairless dog still searches for stale food
on the politician's face in
the newspaper.

BEFORE THE DISASTER

After the mosquito bite, it is another day.
The wall anticipates new height because of its crevice.
From the crumbled breakwater, we look for our lost date.
That was the sky's colorful premonition when evening lowered its flag.
When you intercepted the message,
why did you still wander in the neon-lighted streets?

Do you still remember?
The figures hurrying to look for places to rest their feet
didn't notice a heavy rusty lock
had hung on the exit to the lane.
It was there not because the flood would come,
nor because that cloud-capped hotel
would spark a fire to be the emblem of time.

Evening was usually beautiful,
which was the most effective ritual to bid farewell to the summer heat.
Someone was catching oily fish on the riverbank.
Someone threw away a letter from the faraway place.
And you followed the long-discarded dried brook
to look for an oblong stone to fill in the gap of childhood.

Following the orbit of the earth, the motive of pigeon
to hit down a fighter plane can be transmitted?
The remains of summer still scattered in the evening tinge.
After supper there were still smiles saying good evening on TV.
After announcing the African famine,
the screen with some gaudy postmodern dresses
drew up the curtain for a multicolor night.

At midnight, you and I sat on the bed,
imbued with flowers' mystic fragrance of autumn outside the window.
The breeze coursed through our bodies.
Tempted to whisper something touching to each other,
eyes closed, we sweetly lay down to the upcoming
giant centennial earthquake.

Translations by the author

ALBERTO MILIÁN

Defying Time and History: An Interview with Ricardo Pau-Llosa

With *The Mastery Impulse,* Ricardo Pau-Llosa has now published five collections of poems. His previous titles are *Vereda Tropical* (1999), *Cuba* (1993), *Bread of the Imagined* (1992), and *Sorting Metaphors* (winner of the first Anhinga Prize in 1983). In addition to his work as a poet, he is one of the premier art critics on Latin American art; a guest curator at the Lima Biennial; author of major critical texts on Olga de Amaral, Rafael Soriano, Clarence Holbrook Carter, Rogelio Polesello, Fernando de Szyszlo, and Cuban art in exile; and contributor to many art magazines, including *Art International* magazine, at which he held a decade-long position as a senior editor. Pau-Llosa's short fiction has also been well received and anthologized.

Despite his presence in anthologies and special issues of magazines dedicated to Latinos and his passionate identification with "old Cuba" (as he refers to Cuba before Castro), there is no way of seeing him or his work as ethnic. He is a consummate poet of reflection, as much at home with German philosophy as with pre-Columbian artifacts.

The home he shares with his wife, Morella, in Coral Gables, Florida, is a veritable museum of modern, contemporary, folk, and tribal art, and reflects the hedonism of his poetry, as well as the luxury of his mind and appetites, not least of which is his penchant for fine cigars, the incense of which is ubiquitous. He is a sophisticated Hispanic Caribbean man of the old school, which is to say he is a witty, self-confident Mediterranean cosmopolitan who is painfully aware of history, madly in love with beauty, and stubbornly romantic in his hope for freedom in his native Cuba and justice in his beloved Latin America.

The following interview was conducted over three sessions during the weekend of 2 to 4 November 2001 at the poet's home.

AM Tell me about your childhood and what events or aspects of it influenced your becoming a poet.

RPLl The problem with the "influence" [*gestures quotation marks with fingers*] is that the last person who can truly determine it is the one suffering it. I come from a family that rose, through tremendous hard work, from poverty, when I was born, to middle-class status by the time I was six. That was in Havana during a period most Americans see in only the bleakest nightmare terms because it was the time of Fulgencio Batista's dictatorship [1952–1958]. Despite the political crisis in which the young Cuban republic always found itself in, Batista—who was a dictator and a crook—ruled during a time of great economic and cultural expansion in Cuba. It would come to be known as Cuba's golden age, despite his dictatorship, and unfortunately I was born at that time and not twenty years earlier so that I could have enjoyed it as an adult.

AM But what specific aspects of your childhood—

RPLl These *are* the aspects. It's not just about the kind of house I lived in, or the school I went to, or the kind of parents and siblings I had, or what religion or what toys, what TV shows I watched. It has always been, for me, a question of the dense historical juncture into which I was born. That awareness shaped my life as an adult and most certainly has impacted my work and emerged many times in it as a theme. The reality of that Cuba into which I was born and would be expelled from at the age of six is made all the more dramatic by the complete distortion with which most Americans—indeed, most Cubans my generation or younger—view that period of Cuban history. The facts speak for themselves: Cuba was the only nation that was modern in style, outlook, and dynamism, and Latin American in essence. Indeed, more than any other country in the region, Cuba shaped what everyone has come to think of as Latin American, and it did this through its music, its attitude toward life, and its pioneering literature and visual arts. The loss of this unique homeland was at that time, when I was six, very painful for me, and has become only more so with time.

AM You would say, then, that exile and the loss of homeland influenced you to become a writer.

RPLl Indirectly, perhaps, yes. Indirectly in that I was immersed in an environment—first in Chicago, then Tampa—that was not only completely different from Havana, but the people I encountered had no idea where I came from. Later I would come to realize this was an experience I shared with all immigrants who came to America—the "old country" could just as well have been Mars, as far as most Americans were concerned. Most of them knew nothing about the rest of the world, and despite cable TV, the Internet, and travel, most still don't. Later, when I was fourteen, we moved to Miami—my family and I, my parents, a sister four years older than I, and my maternal grandmother. My father died of a heart attack ten years ago, but my ninety-six-year-old grandmother, a tough *asturiana* [from a province in northern Spain], is still with us, in great health and lucid.

AM So the culture shock of coming to America, made all the more intense because you were a six-year-old, impacted your future development as an artist. But how, exactly, do you feel that influence or impact occurred?

RPLl The first contact, as it were, with America would, unfortunately, become a paradigm that would repeat itself countless times and still does. I found I had to explain the world I came from because others could not form a picture of me without a sense of that world; and because they had a dim or distorted sense of that world, their view of me would also be dim or distorted. Had I found an environment where my "otherness" [*gestures the quotation marks*] was of no consequence, where I was accepted or rejected for purely personal or routine reasons, then the image the natives had of my origins, however inaccurate or simplistic, would not have been an issue in their dealings with me and, consequently, Cuba would have melted away in my child's mind. It probably would have become a place I had been born in but not one I was attached to. Ironically, many Cuban Americans who were brought up in Miami or New Jersey—surrounded by other Cuban exiles and their descendants—have become assimilated in the classical sense; they lost all links to the old country. Although they grew up in a much more Cuban environment, say in southwest Miami, or *because* they grew up in this environment, they see Cuba as a vague, distant point of origin. They are not inspired or driven by it or its history, and least of all by its culture—about which they know close to nothing. They didn't have to Cubanize their sense of themselves to stave off a hostile environment.

AM You said the first contact served as a paradigm, that it would repeat.

RPLl Still does, only the distortion is now ideologically driven. It is no secret that our cultural, academic, and media elites are overwhelmingly supportive of the Castro regime and exhibit a knee-jerk antagonism toward its exiles. This became glaringly obvious during the Elián saga. The internal pro-democratic dissident movement, operating under extreme suppression inside Cuba, is utterly ignored by these liberal or progressive folks, who have championed similar dissidents struggling against right-wing governments. For these people, my position as a vocal opponent of the Castro regime is a source of mystery, dread, or revulsion. Recently, in an article on Miami, Jonathan Kandell, a former *New York Times* correspondent writing for *Cigar Aficionado*, referred to me as "the rarest of specimens" because I am both a poet and an anti-communist. This coincidence of artist and anti-communism amazed him. Later, in correspondence, I pointed out to him that the only pro-communist or anti-anti-communist artists and intellectuals are those who have never experienced that system in any way, shape, or form, but who have read its propaganda. More significantly, they endorse such tyrannical states because it enhances their radical-chic image—hence facilitates their professional status as artists and intellectuals here, in the U.S., a capitalist democracy that nurtures them. This is a source of distortion about Cuban history and culture that is not based on ignorance but on calculated maneuver, on the willingness of cognizant individuals to use the suffering of a defenseless people and don a political disguise in order to advance their own interests.

AM But getting back to the cultural, as opposed to a political, sense of these things, you feel Cuban and not American, although you've lived here for forty-one of your forty-seven years?

RPLl It's not that simple! I am no longer Cuban, that's obvious. The Cuba I am speaking of—the one I had to reconstruct and preserve, and read up on, and experience mostly through the stories and accounts of elders—perished in the early sixties. Were I to go to Cuba today, it would no doubt be a very foreign place, more so than other Latin American countries, which have evolved and changed in a more normal way. Cuba, thanks to its government and system, is a totally bizarre reality, a once-modern nation reduced to feudalism in the name of socialist progress. Of course, I don't belong to that Cuba and may never belong in any future Cuba, either. I live a kind of dual citizenship—my lifestyle is American, and my imagination is Cuban, or old Cuban.

AM But didn't your education in America, the fact that you write in English and teach and live here, have *any* influence on that imagination? Didn't the writers you read and studied who were American have any impact?

RPLl Of course they did. What a question! You are assuming Cuba and America have impermeable boundaries. Cuba was a very Americanized place, and a very Latin place. In other words, had there been no communist takeover more than four decades ago, and I had grown up in the country of my birth, there might not have been such a huge difference between the man I am now, culturally speaking, and the one I would have become. The duality of which I speak would have been possible, albeit in a different form, had Cuba not plunged into totalitarianism. The old Cuba also deeply influenced America, and her absence had a negative effect on America, too. Cuba had a lunar relationship with America, tugging at the uptight, Protestant American psyche and infecting America with a sense that pleasure was not only OK but essential. Had there been a Cuba–U.S. link during the sixties, that period might have been less convulsive in America, less drug-crazed and self-destructive, for Cuba was the role model for America's budding hedonism after World War II. Cuba functioned in some ways as America's anima. Americans today have reduced this view to a caricature: pre-communist Cuba as brothel. Ironically, it has been the communists who have turned Cuba into a premier spot for teen prostitution en masse. Nonetheless, often in the sphere of cultural criticism we speak as if cultures were encased in themselves and a person in one country can only absorb the culture of another by moving to it and living in it. This is a central tenet in the American mythology of immigration, yet it is a woefully simplistic view of cultural interaction.

AM What American writers influenced you, especially in your college years, which, I would assume, is when you began to commit yourself to the writer's life?

RPLl The list would sound like that of many others, for one can't help but be influenced by the masters, the canon, especially the great writers in the language in which you are launching your creative efforts. In high school I loved García Lorca. Wallace Stevens, during my college days, was the American writer whom I read with most interest. I wrote my master's thesis on Stevens, and for a while thought I would write my dissertation on his work as well. I admired Stevens as a poet-thinker, as someone who made no distinctions between philosophy and poetry. Later, it would be Hart Crane, James Dickey, Richard Wilbur, and Derek Walcott. All the while I was also reading Spanish and Latin American writers: Pablo Neruda, César Vallejo, and Jorge Luis Borges in particular—Borges for the same reason I admired Stevens. In fact, I had the opportunity to visit Borges at his home in Buenos Aires in August 1985, about a year before his death. And I mentioned to him that what I most admired in his poems was precisely that they seemed like thoughts caught in the mind of the thinker, and that this was a translucent quality I hoped my work would attain someday. I think it was the only thing I managed to say the whole morning that he seemed pleased with. At any rate, I was influenced by philosophers and historians as much as, if not more than, by poets. And by painters and sculptors, too.

AM Which philosophers and historians do you think influenced you?

RPLl Edmund Husserl, the father of modern phenomenology and its subsequent spin-offs, existentialism among them, has been and continues to be the greatest influence on my work as a poet and as an art critic. It took forever for me to feel like I had gotten his ideas, and I am by no means a scholar of his work. I can only nibble at his light. But I kept at it because I realized that he was the watershed, the true creator of what we think of as modernity in the world of ideas. Through Husserl I got into Heidegger for a while, and Merleau-Ponty, but Husserl is the enduring giant. I loved reading history; while in college I read for content—classical and medieval history of Europe especially. With time I came to savor the style of the historian as much if not more than the focus of his tale. Fernand Braudel's *The Mediterranean World in the Age of Philip II*. Thucydides. Tacitus. Gibbon. I loved Frances Yates's book *The Art of Memory* because it gave memory a space, a history, and a shape. Memory itself may well be an art as much as a faculty of the mind. Memory theaters…I feel I've been building and living in one all my life. Among the modern philosophers of ethics—apart from Albert Camus—the Russian Nicholas Berdyaev is important to me. His book *Slavery and Freedom* is monumental. He is an ignored moral genius.

AM Why Husserl? Can you go into more detail on his influence?

RPLl Husserl's focus on consciousness itself, as the act that embraces world and mind, struck me as wondrous and simple and obvious, yet, because of these qualities, ignored or overlooked for ages. He conceives of awareness as one extension, unbroken by dualism—a field or sphere with two poles that correspond to the old designations of mind and world. The break with dualism that Descartes resisted and Kant pointed to, Husserl brings home. Dualism is the fundamental crack from which many of our great evils come. Without dualism, without that severance between mind and world, the brutality of our religious authorities and ideological leaders would not have been possible. Dualism opens the door, at its very onset in Socrates, to the totalitarian prototype of his Republic. The breach between mind and world mirrors the gulf between man and God in Judaism and Christianity. It is a breach that must be filled by faith and what attends to faith—intolerance, orthodoxy, liturgy, hierarchies of authority in spiritual matters, all that arrogance of soul we call religion. Dualism is the manna of the messianic tyrant. Husserl took consciousness as the parameter of reality, the base of his epistemology. His is a philosophy that elucidates continuity, takes it as premise, because it's not about the presence of the world in the mind, but about the inextricable presence of both in consciousness. Husserl's foregrounding of consciousness would include our consciousness of the past, our memories, and the accounts of others. Intersubjectivity itself. That is why Husserl was so valuable in my approach to Cuba.

What Cuba was historically and culturally can be reconstructed from data, even from the evidence of what's left after forty-two years of communist tyranny and imbecilic destruction. Havana, for example, is still a wondrous place, a city built by immigrants and by its bustling middle class from the early thirties through the fifties. That's not the only Cuba I am speaking of, however. Cuba as a context for an imagination and a place from which many great artists emerged simultaneously is another Cuba altogether. That Cuba isn't so easy to subject to suspensions, reconstitutions, or other self-reflective cognitive acts. That Cuba is still alive, is still feeding the imaginations of those who tap into it. When a place becomes what I call a renaissance point, it doesn't die, or doesn't have to. It becomes a nurturing confluence of creative possibilities, a way of dialoguing with identity and fate and the mysteries of life itself. It becomes a language, a logic, a set of rules for the creative imagination to come to life in and through. But that language can't be activated unless the historical Cuba is clarified, because an artist enters that language with heart and mind and imagination, and not just intellectually. Perhaps the death of Cuba as a culture was the beginning of its life as timeless renaissance point. Or perhaps it was the senseless and sudden and cruel nature of that death, for had the Cuban renaissance petered out, that descent might have diluted its presence. Indeed, Cuba is Firenze-like in that way, Minoan. A burst of light, then a sudden darkness brought on by the implacable if fortuitous triumph of chaos.

AM Is the idea of old Cuba as "a renaissance point" related to the often-cited opening sentence of your essay on Cuban art in *Outside Cuba/Fuera de Cuba*: "Every exile knows his place, and that place is the imagination"?

RPLl Somewhat, I guess. That sentence, which Gustavo Pérez Firmat has cited and commented on but has not really gotten, is a simpler statement. It plays with the cliché of knowing one's place, poignant for the exile who is not at all a native and is made to feel not as good as one. The exile is always aware of his condition as an escapee from a culture that failed terribly in some way, unless he is a refugee from an invasion or occupation—a different kind of exile. There's the guilt survivor and the heroic survivor. The place the exile makes his own is possible by activating one of the highest functions of the imagination, the act of belonging, but in this case it is indistinguishable from reviving and possessing. One belongs to freedom, not to a place, but it needs place as a compass needs north. I'm not talking about a passive, feel-good, or fuzzy membership in a legacy, or the kind of strident ethno-babble that passes as multiculturalism these days. In this sense, the place of the exile is the memory theater that focuses all that is known about a condition and its history, and puts it at the service of wisdom, for lack of a less-mangled word. Exilic imagining is a defiance of history, as true creative imagining is a defiance of time. More precisely, exilic imagining at the service of creativity unites both defiances.

AM Can you explain how all this might have influenced the conception or execution of particular poems?

RPLl What is cause and what is effect is hard to say. I'm not sure either of these analogies is to the point. I didn't want to write riddles, nor did I want Neruda-type odes to everyday things, although both of these influenced what I was experimenting with. I wanted the poem to capture the processes of suspension and reconstitution simultaneously, or superimpose them. Now, these are poems about perceptions in anyone's everyday world. The exilic dimension came through for me in the poems of my third book, *Cuba*. You asked for particular poems. From that collection, I would point to "Frutas" as a poem about perception and intersubjectivity, although for some it is a poem about the latina grandmother and nostalgia. Yuck! Yes, my grandmother is the protagonist, along with the *mamey* [a rare tropical fruit] we are tasting after many years in exile not having had a *mamey*. But "Frutas" is my parody of Plato's Cave, and self-parody too. The poem is making fun of the very enterprise at the heart of the book, the recovery of Cuba as an act of the imagination. It ends with the boy persona failing to adjust the real *mamey* before him to the fabulous *mameyes* of old Cuba the grandmother is recalling. He is exiled, for a second time, from his grandmother's range of experiences. He is made to realize that they are not and never can be his because every act of consciousness, even a shared one like this *mamey*, is unique to the subject enacting it. Husserl referred to what we share in experience as the life-world or *lebenswelt*. At the end the boy's questioning the grandmother leads to an abrupt answer that unveils what has been going through her head, as opposed to his innocent or childish endeavor to reconstruct a "real" *mamey* from her recollection of the old days. "Next you'll want to know how we lost a country" is her unveiling of how exiled she feels—again—in the face of this not-quite-good-enough fruit. He can't get this. No going home again, not even for dessert. Of course, the grandmother is also dismissing Plato and his realm of ideas.

AM You mention the visual artists, and you have published extensively on Latin American art. How has the art you've studied impacted your poetry, and vice versa?

RPLl The vice versa is everything in this matter. As I write an essay about an artist's work, I will also be spinning off poems based on the images, or sometimes I start with poems and when these are more or less done, I feel the need to write an essay to clarify concepts the poems can't accommodate. They are complementary approaches to the issue of intersubjectivity, only the other subjective realm before me is already present through images and tropes as a work of art. It is not, in other words, another person whose inner life I must intend. When dealing with paintings as a poet, I must create another work of art capable of being "had," as a dream is had, as a painting is had and not just seen, independently of the painting that triggered it. That is one reason I have chosen to write poems based on works by Latin American artists who are largely unknown in the U.S. I am obviously very familiar with these works and the traditions that inform them, but their anonymity to the poetry reader presents a greater challenge than writing poems about famous European or North American artists. It also enables the reader to intend the poem rather than the poem-painting duality.

AM   In what way do you see the artist as being different from nonartists?

RPL1 If we're talking here about the genuine artist, rather than the careerists who have come to dominate all aspects of cultural life in the developed world, then the artist is different in countless ways. The artist *is*, he doesn't *do*. That is, art is a complete giving over of oneself to what one creates. Yet the artist's life—whatever images it may provide—is of little consequence to the work itself. He cannot inhabit his art, for that dwelling privilege belongs to those who come to his art, who wish to have this art in their minds. It is the height of rudeness for the artist to be seen still in his art when someone else is trying to move into that house. This doesn't mean at all that the poet cannot use his own experiences and memories, only that they must be used to serve the general theater of transmission involved in someone else having the poem.

Paradoxically, only the artist can sustain his identity as public force, for his public may not be his contemporaries. There is a great deal to be said for the old system in which artists very consciously worked to change the way the future saw its present and its past—and did not work so much to obtain prestige and accolades in the artist's lifetime. Ironically, artists have continued to pursue the old dependencies on patrons, although these come in the form of academic positions or other forms of support from politically defined groups, invariably of the Left. This has produced a monstrous careerist artist type in our time: the opportunist who pretends to be an independently minded professional but who will do whatever, say whatever to secure the support of his patrons. The result is a careerist who justifies his utter lack of political ethics, who disdains the masses he often pretends to speak up for, and who will quickly align himself with fashionable tyrannies while denouncing only what his faction decides is worthy of denunciation. It is precisely in the realm of civic behavior and ethics where the artist is no different from anyone else, yet it is in this realm where it has become acceptable for artists in our time to differ most radically from other people.

AM Are you a bitter man?

RPLl I am not whining, if that's what you mean. I don't whine. I denounce.

AM Can you expound on what you mean by "theater," a word you have used often in this conversation and, I feel, means various things to you?

RPLl I have used that word to describe Latin American visual thinking, particularly the refusal of this tradition to look at representation in negative terms, as occurred in the North, for example, and in many different schools and movements in European modernism. Modernism, or as it is called in Latin America, *la vanguardia,* sought to broaden the power of representation in painting, not bracket it. The result is a modernism whose paintings are theatrical in that they consciously put images in play, in action among themselves, borrowing from plot and narrative a reverberative sense of meaning, but not really telling a story as it were—something pretty hard to do with painting, as Diego Rivera's obtuse murals evidence. Theater, then, denotes a cognizant ambition of the work of art to dramatize ideas. It is most salient in painting, that of Latin America especially, because of how different this makes it from parallel movements elsewhere in the West. But it is a reality also in all poetry where the break with representation did not occur except in the curiously named LANGUAGE experimenters, whom I don't think of as poets. They're retro-Dada and remind me of many so-called conceptual visual artists who have no concepts. Still, North American poets are not great at embracing the theater of the poem, the sense that you can inhabit the poem, that it gives you a habitat for mind, senses, imagination, and memory. Latin American art gave me that sense, that need in the poem. That—and not the triggering or inspiration a painting might provide as a launching pad for a poem—is the most important lesson I have taken from the world of the visual arts, as a poet.

AM I would like you to conclude with comments on what comes after *The Mastery Impulse* and on where the art criticism is taking you.

RPLl The art writing is always going on. I've just finished a long essay that will be coming out in a book on Nicolás Leiva, and have several articles coming out in art magazines. I am nearing completion of a collection of poems, written in both Spanish and English, which I've begun to publish pieces of in magazines. It is titled *Crab* and it consists of short poems set on a beach, and whose protagonist—there's the theater metaphor again—is a crab. These poems began in Spanish, which is the first time since I was a teenager that I've written poems in my native language, although I have written many articles in Spanish, lectured, etcetera. Then I translated some of them into English, then wrote others in English and translated those into Spanish. At some point, and this happens when you are translating your own work, you really are writing in both languages at once, or with awareness of both simultaneously, as you are making corrections that reverberate in one tongue to the other. I am also working on a collection of poems that I am dedicating to my wife, Morella, a wonderful *venezolana* who has connected me to nature and living in all sorts of new ways. Left to my own impulses, I'd never leave the city. She's taken me into the high Andes, the Amazons, virgin beaches in the Caribbean, into deserts and jungles. I who dread heights, who cannot climb past the second rung on a ladder, have walked cheerfully behind her, through waterfalls in Canaima in the Amazons. As an art collector of many years, she's also taught me a thing or two about appreciating art, and of course everything about love, kindness, and patience. I follow her studiously in all the things that matter about living, and I've come to see that attitude as the only certain sign of love.

AM   What does your wife, Morella, make of your work, especially the new poems in which she figures?

RPLl She puts up with my cigars, and smokes one herself every now and then.

Immigrant Parable:
Hong Kong Orchid Tree, Arguments

for Ann Rose

> *Things stand outside our door, themselves by themselves, neither*
> *knowing nor reporting anything about themselves. What then*
> *does report about them? The governing self.*
>
> MARCUS AURELIUS

1

Like most trees that spend
their gorgeous efforts
on flowering, these have bitten
leaves and stripped twigs
that cling to branches and whip,
and mold-embroidered trunks.
They rise above perennial beds
of seedless refuse where vermin thrive
until the wind scatters the dead rattling.
It lifts the sunless dirt that haloed
the roots where once grass sprung.
How unnatural, too, these trees,
foreign and dragged onto this soil
to decorate at first, but soon to crowd
flora millennial weathers had tuned
like invisible violins. How they bully
the canopies, tangle the phone lines
and refuse to feed the venerable jay
and the citizen oriole.
Even their blooms are *like* the orchid
but cannot root in air and moisture
nor hold the branches harmless,
nor perfume the shade with hormonal fevers.

Behold how orchids paint their borrowed corners
with strokes of lust, but how these lumberings
breach sidewalk and plumbing
and will not a single true orchid host.
I doubt it is by nature's law—
more the force that keeps the real
from the imagined, and both from the mask.

2

It sturdied the wilting ground and shaded
the fly-strewn air. It spread in exponents
like a rhyme foretold by its doubling leaves,
and so it breathed geometry and pinned
its violet petals where only grasses grew,
the spiked palmetto, and the bleeding sandspur.
Unlike the melaleuca, it left untouched
water's balancing of earth and did not forget
the riding lessons of the typhoon.
Observe the more abundant bee and hummingbird,
the plentiful jars that grace the humblest sills,
the lovers who gather its sighs, and the oils
that emblem the painted tree for the place.
It bore beauty and magnitude onto a flat
murky plain and it unveiled
the languid shapely orchid where none here bloomed.
All its splendid brethren too are new—
hibiscus and heliconia, bougainvillea and bamboo.
It vies with araguaney for the bannering joys
but slips into half-naked sleep when poinciana
bursts into annual flame. It braves the fungus
and the termite and the saw. It knows its function
is to become the object of admired mistrust.

Four Poems

IN THE OUT-OF-THE-WAY CORNERS OF OUR LIVES

so many poems inhabit the out-of-the-way corners of our lives
they've probably never applied to the Census Administration
    Office for a residence permit
or obtained a door plate from a district administration office or a
    police station
as you come walking out of the alleyway, you bump into a jogger
    speaking on his cell phone
his awkward smile reminds you of the old doctor who helps his
    pretty young
wife polish her red sports car in the driveway each night: actually,
these are two stanzas of a much longer poem

tact but no contact between one thing and another
some float to the surface and become images, courting
other images. sounds and scents are usually the first to seduce,
    secretly
exchanging information. colors are bashful young girls, they have
    to stay at home
arranging the curtains bedspreads bathrobes tablecloths waiting for
    their lord and master to come back and switch on
the light. a poem, like a home, is a honeysweet burden
where love desire pain sadness are housed, sameness and difference
    accommodated

they don't need to go off to the clinic to have their tubes tied or buy
    condoms
even though they have a morality and a family planning all of their
    own
socio-economic compatibility doesn't necessarily make for the best
    matches
and while it's true milk can be mixed with water, fire and water can
    be mated too

Whitehead eats blackbird, a black-headed fly argues
    philosophically that
a white horse be no horse at all. tender violation
a deafening silence
forbidden love is the special prerogative of poetry

some of them choose to live in the shadow
    of metaphors or in forests of symbols
some are cheerful and optimistic, climbing
    everywhere like spiders of
sunshine. others prefer to eat the wind and
    drink the dew, talk pure talk and have
illicit sex, others resemble invisible gauze
scattered in your brain subdivided into so
    many suites of rooms for rent,
    occasionally
starting up the looms of dream and
    unconsciousness
so many poems apparently imprisoned in
    rooms of habitual action. you shut
    your door
looking for words, rifling through boxes
    and cupboards, imploring, you even
    ride inspiration's electric donkey
driving the mouse, pressing down keys
    and conducting searches. open a
    window
the big wide world, that's where you find
    them:
irises after rain. a flock of seagulls
on its way home from school. an oblique
    patterning
of ripples in the sea
a pot of tomatoes with a few squares of
    beancurd cooking in the microwave

*"Electric donkey" is a reference to
the poet Li He (A.D. 790–816), who
supposedly often searched for inspi-
ration on his family estate while
mounted on a donkey*

you remember you still need some peas. as you walk into the
    supermarket you see
TIN CAN   TIN CAN   TIN CAN   TIN CAN   TIN CAN   TIN CAN   TIN CAN
TIN CAN   TIN CAN   TIN CAN   TIN CAN   TIN CAN   TIN CAN   TIN CAN
TIN CAN   TIN CAN   TIN CAN   TIN CAN   TIN CAN   TIN CAN   TIN CAN
you reach out and take down a can only to find that this tin you've
    wracked
your brains over, that you spent so much effort tracking down,
    owes its

whole existence to an absence:

TIN CAN	TIN CAN	TIN CAN	TIN CAN	TIN CAN	TIN CAN	TIN CAN
TIN CAN	TIN CAN	TIN CAN		TIN CAN	TIN CAN	TIN CAN
TIN CAN	TIN CAN	TIN CAN	TIN CAN	TIN CAN	TIN CAN	TIN CAN

a solitary persimmon on the counter. you say
How splendid! a solitary persimmon on the counter
now there's a line with a style all of its own
you can't help suspecting it's an immigrant from Japan or the T'ang
　　dynasty, renowned for its quatrains
but you don't mind at all. don't mind at all that they all fit inside
one small shopping bag

KUBLA KHAN

in Xanadu did Kubla Khan
a vast, mobile pleasure-dome decree
"I don't want anything fixed. Although I've got hundreds and
　　thousands of imperial concubines
I'm sick and tired of them
installed in their fixed apartments, using their fixed perfumes
moaning after going through the fixed formulas…"
his Italian consultant, an adept in the field of business management,
　　made careful selections, devised meticulous plans
dividing these damsels into various groupings, either groups of six or
　　teams of three or four or five
three nights at a time, adopting different positions and a variety of
　　formations
they took turns to minister to their lord

fine wines, opium, honey, leather whips
terrestrial globes, vibrators, sacred texts, kinky lingerie
"I want constant motion, constant stimulation, constant conquest,
constant orgasm…"

but this was in no sense a mathematical problem
nor a military one, not even a medical one

outside the dome a Persian traveller who had been overlooked for
　　the important job said,
"This is a philosophical issue.
Time is the best aphrodisiac
for the conception of change"

FOIL CARTON

drink me
drink my blood
drink my milk
drink the saliva from my mouth
drink the juices of my body
drink the fluids of my love
drink my spasms my convulsions
drink my infidelity

before the use-by date expires
(for date of manufacture, see bottom of casket)

BUTTERFLY-MAD

here she comes in my direction
looking like a butterfly. without hesitation
she sits down directly in front of the lectern
in her hair, a bright-colored
hair clip: butterfly on butterfly

in the past twenty years, in this junior high
by the sea, how many butterflies have I seen
shaped like human beings, like butterflies
carrying youth, carrying dreams, flut-
tering into my classrooms?

oh, Lolita

one autumn day before noon, the sunlight
so warm, a dazzling Yellow
flew in through the window and circled
between the distracted teacher
and a thirteen-year-old girl concentrating on her schoolwork

suddenly, she was up on her feet
trying to hide from that scissory shimmering color-
shape, a butterfly terrified of
other butterflies: she, startled by
them; me, perplexed by their beauty

Translations by Simon Patton

Three Poems

DON'T YOU FEEL THE MORNING BECOMES HER?

for Yan for a Senegalese woman

Don't you feel
The morning becomes her?
Don't you feel that it becomes her?
Running
For instance

Opening an old cookie tin becomes her
Reading all the old damp letters
She is the very image of a cork
In a wine bottle. Don't you feel that
Bolting 'cross a starry sky becomes her?
Having a will of her own becomes her
And other things become her too. For instance
A graceful fall becomes her

Don't you feel that you could rub her right away
She is just that kind of ink
But then you find her thumbprint reappearing right before your eyes

Don't you feel that
Rubbing becomes her?
Don't you feel that
Coming in the morning becomes her?

SCENARIO FOR A TANGO

Our story opens on a converted river barge lost in mist
Where we find our protagonist who makes this barge her home
Hard at work on a romantic horror thriller
She had started out to write a sort of "Grand Guignol"
But the romantic interests of the story wound up
Taking over until the air of horror
All but disappeared

Drifting down the long inland waterways she often docks at some
Little town or other to post the new installments of her novel
(Did I mention it was a serial?) or replenish her stores or stories
And every time she runs across someone who strikes her fancy
She invites them to join her on the river where she pries from them
Their most passionate and terrifying experience
But whenever the storytellers start to bore her she lures them
    to the railing
And drowns them in the river where the water runs deep

Now and then her story drifts into shamelessly racy waters
But each time she manages to pilot a chapter safely into port
She turns to that imagined voyeur with a *"Schmilblick avance!"*
And so moving on we find her vessel listing in the waves until
Her words incline to sweeping themes her story is set adrift
Conversations left piled upon the rocks characters lost at sea
And we cut to terra firma to find our heroine
Fairly hurrying to the dentist

Close-up of the writer sitting in a dental waiting room
Filling out an order form for an encyclopedia she found
Flipping through the latest issue of *Voyeur*
Any moment may find her tempting the unsuspecting
Stranger to step on board to tell their tale unless of course…
But then we are familiar with her modus operandi

Even the river can find neither head nor heels of
All those people she literally wrote off but
When her tale is done her boat emerges from the spectral fog
And the spirits of those many artless storytellers gather round
Lay hands to oars and with one great breath fill her sails
And set her craft in motion

How the many murderous devices authored in this all-too-lyrical
    tango
Have led our heroine off the straight and narrow to the mouth
Of this river where in the guise of a wolf she gazes out into the offing
And we track to the familiar face of the water in which once again we
See those astonished victims drowning in her inverted reflection
As it morphs into the very image of a wolf
Howling for its mate

A PERSONAL HELL

to Borges

When sleepwalkers chance to
Come across each other their dreams
Intermingle like two clouds converging
And it rains and one of the sleepers
Wakes inside a room and
Opens his eyes and says: "It is raining"
Never knowing that his nocturnal wanderings have landed him in
Some other person's home wearing some other person's shoes
Which for some odd reason fit as snugly as his own
Wearing some other person's clothes sitting down to breakfast
At some other person's table with some other person's significant
    other
Never knowing that he himself has become an other
And while there are surely some among his friends and family
Who have come to harbor certain vague suspicions that he is not
The person he appears to be nothing ever comes of this
As such suspicions seem part of the general irreality
Nor will he ever come to know that it is the shoes that sustain
    the illusion
For wouldn't you know if the shoes you were wearing were not
    your own?
Thus are we each persuaded every morning when we rise
Won over by the shoes and the rest it never occurs to us
We are no longer quite ourselves
And the uncanny part of this is that
The reason why other people's shoes
Always seem to fit so well is that as long as
There is but one of us still fast asleep
The rest of us live on inside the dream

Translations by Steve Bradbury

Six Poems

TREE MID-TREE

the at-the-eyelash tree much happiness
at mid-look, the tree in the fog
at the fog's finger a stirring earlobe
the earlobe's toothgap so the tongue sticks out

the at-the-nose bridge tree true peace & calm
at mid-sniff, the tree amid wind
at wind's skirt hem stirring short whiskers
the short whiskers at the lip so the nose sticks out

the at-the-hairline tree much radiance
at mid-weep, the tree in the rain
at the rain's foot & leg stirring cheekbones
the cheekbones at the temples so the long hair sticks out

at mid-eye there are little stars in the fog
at mid-dew, at the slight tremble
at mid-ear there's a small river in the rain
at mid-wind, at lowered tear

at mid-hand there's fog in an armbend
at mid-hair there's wind in between neck and collar
there's rain on the face
there's dew at the nose bridge
there's a stream in the valley
there's a road at the stream bank
there's a tree in the woods
there's a heart on the tree
at mid-tree at mid-tree
at mid-tree, there's a tree extreme regret

tree among tree
tree amid tree
that tree mid-tree *ha!*

STAND SIGN

This is just fucking nuts! How could they repaint the bus-stand sign
the color of a papaya? As I reach the stand, shouting, I can't keep
from thinking this. Maybe they only have circular signs like this in the
suburbs. Or maybe, in the Transit Authority, there's a poet.

After all, what comes and goes is not what you are waiting for; the one
you wait for, as usual, doesn't come. I would need only stand this
weary body of mine against the signpost to see in the dark of the eyes
a vividly empty, opalescently new vehicle roll out.

I don't know why the bus-stand sign gets lower and lower, nor why it
incrementally evaporates with my body following, unceasingly sink-
ing up to my back, touching the horizon line, when at last my beauti-
ful daughter brings me around by saying: *Ba, the sun's already behind
the mountain.*

Translations by Ryan T. Scott Nance

FLYING GARBAGE

written on Earth Day, 1998

A gust rises.

First, a piece of old newspaper overturned, yesterday's news, today's
history, sent to the other side of the street to be trampled on once
again; then a plastic bag with pink stripes, almost transparent, float-
ing up to the sky, brushing the high-rise of Taiwan Electricity Com-
pany along the way, people following its stumble with their eyes; now
it heads south along Xindian Spring, breaking up a flock of pigeons
before it enters the mountainous region of Five Streams, causing a
falcon to take flight and survey in alert while avoiding in haste the
clamors and sighs of humans, animals, cockroaches in the bag.

The garbage bag continues its journey toward White Cock Hill, ver-
milion clouds write giant characters in the western sky.

FLYING TEARS

Empty mountain, no man in sight.

In the dense fern shrubs, an electric saw growls impudently, squirrels screech among the high branches, bats spread out their fleshy wings, the white tips of their noses tremble more violently than the quaking boughs, the dragon claws of twigs and branches, the phoenix wings of canopies of the trees, all dance frantically in fright, aslant in the howls of the electric saw. Time, one century, three centuries, one thousand years, turns into sawdust dancing in the air. Time, one millennium, two millennia, falls down with a clap of thunder. The past falls down, the future falls down.

Bright green blood flows from the broken grasses.
Carrying tiny umbrellas of white down afar to sow seeds of sorrow.
Dandelions are flying tears.

CLOVER BOMBS

A clover that had escaped the scorching sun was pulled up from under the shady fern shrub by a coarse hand; dark green leaves each made up of three hearts, tiny lilac flowers tinted with yellow. Wanna taste autumn? Tart? A little. Sweet? A little. Best to pin it on the bosom with a milky fragrance. Immediately it's pressed by another bosom, mouths chattering, necks entwined, flowers and leaves flattened, the cone-shaped berries ripen gradually as they are warmed by two people's body heat. The instant the bodies part, the berries explode; not only is there an inaudible cry of joy, but the tiny greenish seeds and tender autumnal sadness are planted deeply in the hearts of this woman and that man.

SUNSHINE ON THE OTHER SIDE OF EARTH

The phone rang
In the ring is the sunshine on the other side of Earth
But we sit in its shadow
Gaze up at the Scorpion of an unruly heart
The Hunter tiptoeing across the firmament
On the other side of Earth no one can see
His belt studded with three bright stars

In the phone ring is a prairie
A grasshopper rides on the breeze across ten miles
A taxi startles a cat at the mouth of the alley
Searching for food in a torn-open garbage bag
In the city where I live
Some yellowed photos are run over by automobile tires

On the other side of Earth is a telephone
Sunlight spreads coldness
The temperature keeps dropping
A cool hand placed on
The shoulder like a turntable losing speed
Counting lingering notes after a power shortage
Slow, confusing reflections of the carousel
In the light of the candle with a curled-up wick
A glitter in the eye
Wondering if the phone ever rang at all

Translations by Michelle Yeh

Four Poems

FAX MACHINE

■ Through the fax machine, the world becomes the unworld

Because she misses him, she decides to fax fragrant and sexy red lips across a great distance.

The man sleeps as faxed lips leap from the machine, crawl across the carpet and, trying to climb into his cozy bed, fall and drown in the half-full glass of wine left over from the night before.

She faxes again, this time two streams of tears, real as can be, that are blown dry by the *aircon* as they try to leap from the machine.

She waits for the man's reply and, without it, finally resolves to fax over her own reproachful eyes.

The eyes are faxed over and immediately leap from the machine, scamper across the carpet, climb into the bed—

Finally she sees: beside the man lies a living, breathing woman.

TEETH

■ Moral teachings pick their teeth with human bones as they eat
their way through history

The old man puts in his dentures, picks up a foot-long stick of sugar-cane from the fruit basket and, turning it horizontally, starts munching. Within 3 minutes the sugarcane once hard as a bamboo stick is reduced to wads of fibrous pulp.

"Not a decent one among you, you bunch of rogues and prostitutes. To be blunt, from childhood on you're just a pack of animals dressed up like people." He picks up a second stick and starts gnawing while continuing his diatribe against the bright-faced, respectful young man in leather shoes and a Western suit.

"We must remember our morals, men must observe the *4 Restraints and 8 Virtues,* and women must follow the *3 Obeisances and 4 Virtues.* The mess of today's society is all because you've forgotten the moral ideal…" He moves on to his third stick of sugarcane. The young man lowers his head, silent.

"In those days a father's word was law; children didn't talk back. Whatever a mother wanted her daughter to do, her daughter did—ah!" The old man, spitting out yet another wad of sugarcane, picks up his fourth stick. The young man's head descends until his face is completely out of view. "One must obey, one must respect age and wisdom. One must follow without conditions, be frugal and hard-working, loyal, pure, mindful of the spirits, must…*tew! tew! tew!*" The old man is up to his ankles in expectorated wads of sugarcane. The young man's hands hang at his side; his face is practically pasted to his chest, like a criminal awaiting sentence.

The old man, lost in reverie, adjusts his dentures, brushes them with his tongue, and gives the young man he's scolding one more once-over. Then, taking advantage of his not being aware, in the blink of an eye he yanks a foot-long bone from the young man's chest and goes at it sideways.

Within just a few minutes, many bones as hard as sticks are crunched and gnawed into wads of fibrous pulp.

ON THE PHONE

In the darkness
A distant you suddenly sheds tears   falling silent
You put the receiver to your chest

In this way
I learn from the sound of your heartbeat
To hear all the news of the universe
To gradually hear   the sound of great waters
    of artillery fire
    of the falling earth

REINCARNATION

Midnight sky
After a repentant downpour
The graveyard grows layers of human-faced peach blossoms
Some gaze towards the future
Others   watch the here and now

Spurred sinful wings of bees and butterflies
Rush in throngs from the virtual world to gather pollen and nectar
Some gathering regret
Others collecting resentment
Both race back to the virtual world beyond the graveyard

Dawn sky
After a revelatory drumming of a tropical wind
The roadside trees at the graveyard's entrance
Bear layers of human-faced fruits
Some like to nod their heads in the rain
Others   like to shake their heads in the wind

Translations by Paul Manfredi

Translations from the Akkadian

The sun is a god.
The mountain is a man.
The ox, grazing, breathes heavily in the heat.

The sun god
calls to the mountain man,
his voice an ox lowing on the altar.

The sun god bleeds light.
The mountain man bathes in its stream.
The ox bows its head, drinks deep.

The sun is a song God sings in fire's tongue
to call forth the mountain at the foot of which lies a man
like a stone ox on the grave of the night.

The sun is a fruit dissolving in the mouth of God.
The mountain is the mother's breast
from which the man cannot wean his suckling ox.

The sun dies. God shuts the vault of his eye.
The mountain crumbles into the sea.
The man wakes under a sky of ice. No ox.

The sun runs to God,
racing over the mountain
like a man distraught in search of his errant ox.

The sun summons God
to the top of the mountain.
The man rides his ox into the village.

The sun is no god.
The mountain, all mountain.
The man cries, "Ox!" The ox lifts his leaden head.

The Cargo

A deep-blue stillness was upon the sea as if this were the earth's last morning and the boat, with its cargo of dead bodies, were on a last voyage toward infinity.

He was in a daze, his mind unable to come to grips with bare facts. He was wrestling with the intrusions of fear and despair, alternating like the crest and trough of the waves on the boundless sea, bearing down on him as if the sheer mass of the sea itself. He wanted to talk about these emotions, about anything at all, but there was no one alive in the world. If there had been seagulls, he could have shouted at them, or better still, cursed them. But no seagulls flew this far. If the earth had been flat, this part of the sea would have been its very edge, appearing before the boat plunged into the abyss. Yet, he was aware, the sun was rising steadily, indifferently.

Asmawil stared again. On the bow, under a green tarpaulin, the huddled bodies were still warm. They were seated as though they were merely suffering from sickness. Their heads were bowed or turned. He did not know why he had them seated. He knew them all by name, by their first names. The one wearing a skullcap was his wife's nephew, bodyguard to the ship's owner. For no conscious reason, he had seated these two next to each other.

The motor launch had been drifting for three hours now. He had stopped the engine when he decided to drag the bodies to the bow. But even after he had put the tarpaulin over the bodies and securely tied its ends to the posts supporting the roof, he did not start the engine. He was in no hurry to reach Siasi, the port of departure, or any island for that matter. He was secure on his boat and, more than at any time in his life, he feared the living more than the dead. He knew what folks believed about a dead body on a boat—that it was accompanied by forty-four evil spirits, and that was why any boat carrying a dead body was a slow boat. But he feared neither the dead nor their spirits. For one thing, they did not ask any questions; or if they did, the questions were never on their lips, only in their eyes, in their faraway stare. They seemed to be looking for something farther than their eyes could see. They seemed to ask, but since their questions were never uttered, he did not have to answer them. Besides, he was certain there were no spirits.

He went to the kitchen at the stern and brewed himself some coffee. He had not realized, until now, how hungry he was. When he sat down to drink his second cup, with a cigarette between his fingers, he imagined what would happen when he got back to Siasi. The whole town would turn out and flock to the wharf to see his cargo. The people would be out on the streets as they would be on a morning when a *hadji* came home from a pilgrimage to Mecca. Except that there would be no school band, no streamers of welcome, no firecrackers, no rich and flowing robes, no turban, no tell-tale bruise on the forehead, which was the true mark of a pilgrim who had kissed the black stone at Kaaba. Because his was a different pilgrimage. Just a night at sea and a boat of ten men, nine of them now dead. As for the bruise, it was nowhere on the body.

And the people would ask all kinds of questions and interrupt themselves with accusations and curses. Did he kill them all? All of them? What a devil! Including his nephew? It's only his wife's nephew. The same. How can anyone do such a thing? He has a tail. Money, all that money. A hundred and fifty thousand, maybe more. More. Abdul was a rich man. No, it was not his; it was the middlemen's. Robber, just the same. They will get his neck. Think of the relatives of the dead. Sure, the sons of Abdul. Why do you think he did it? He has a tail. No, greed. Insanity. They will kill even the cats in his house. Curse upon his children!

Upon my children? He shuddered to think of the curse upon his children. The curse upon his head he was ready to accept. He had seen enough of life and would willingly part with it. He could accept the end of his life the way he accepted that sharp, sudden pain at the back of his head each morning when he woke up. But not the curse of blood upon his children. Never his children. Never his wife. It was not right that they suffer for his sins, whatever those sins were. Besides, he did not do it. His children must not suffer. Neither must he.

For the first time since he was confronted with his cargo, his mind cleared up, and he recalled the incident only several hours before. It seemed ages ago, but when he looked again at the tarpaulin, he recalled that only yesterday afternoon he had seen the longshoremen roll two black, dented barrels of gasoline on a slender gangplank. He had feared the plank would break under the pressure. As a boat pilot for many years, he had seen enough of loading and unloading to know that the plank would only bend. He knew that as well as the longshoremen did. Yet he had some vague fear that the plank would break. Perhaps he had been wishing it would so the trip would have to be delayed. If one of the barrels dropped into the sea, as he had wished, it would have given him a few more hours at home. He could have let the crew worry about it. He would have gone home to be with his wife.

When the last barrel had been rolled safely and staked in place on the side of the deck, one of the longshoremen, fiddling at his goose throat and showing his toothless gum, gave Asmawil a wide grin as if to mock him for his fear and selfish wish. Instead of being relieved, Asmawil was mildly angry and uncomfortable that his wish had not come true. Courteously, he smiled back at the longshoreman, who was still grinning and looking intently at him. Suddenly, something more than anger and frustration seized him. He went inside the poop to blow the horn. Two long, hoarse, and impatient whistles startled the languid sundown, but the afterimage of that grinning face remained. A vague sensation flowed through him like a breath.

The owner of the boat came out of the restaurant with his bodyguard and other members of the crew. A successful trader for some years, Abdul Tungki was a short, corpulent man whose waddling movements were made more pronounced by his bulging back pockets. Whether they were full of money or just business papers, nobody was certain. People who saw him waddle down the street on a busy day assumed that it must be money. As a trader, he made a fortune buying barter goods from Sandakan for the middlemen in Siasi. Even in the days before the national government sanitized the word "contraband" into "barter," Abdul Tungki had always overstuffed his pockets the way most successful businessmen did. It was a status symbol, like carrying a chromium-plated .45, that the new rich should not be denied. They were to be envied, and only the poor bystanders of finer sensibilities were repulsed. On a trip like this, Abdul's bodyguard, slinging an armalite, carried his black attaché case.

Asmawil had come out of the poop and lighted a cigarette. He inhaled the first smoke deeply and blew slowly out into the clear air. He was relieved to know that the weather was fine. It was not dark yet. High in the west the moon was an imperfect crescent. A feeble star hung above one of its horns. A week before, when he and his wife were relaxing on the porch of his house in South Laud, he had noticed that the star was directly above the valley of the crescent, and the moon looked like the crook of a mother's arm cradling an infant. Looking at the moon and the star close together never failed to amuse him because of what folks believed: that the conjunction of these two heavenly bodies meant two young lovers were going to elope. Yet when he himself ran off with his wife, there was no such heavenly sign. He doubted the accuracy of the folk belief, but he was certain that, moon or no moon, young lovers ran off because it was the cheapest way to get married. Their hot blood did not wait for heaven's sanction, nor for any distant signs, only for the encouraging glint in their lover's eyes. The young had common sense. For them, the way through the knot of conventions was not to untie it but to cut it. Also, their acceptance of the risks they incurred when they ran off was somewhat romantic. And Asmawil knew those risks.

He thought of his wife, seven months pregnant and getting heavier every time he came home from Sandakan. He would amuse her by pretending to listen to the vigorous kick of the fetus, and then afterwards he would tickle her by kissing her navel. It was definitely going to be their last, boy or girl. He had promised that to her. He had said the same thing three years before, but when the child turned out to be another boy, he reneged on his promise. He wanted a girl so that he could name her Napsa, after the dancer in a famous story, and he wanted her to be a dancer like her mother.

His wife had been a dancer of no mean fame, but there was no trace of that lithe, willowy girl with whom, many years ago, he had run off on a pump boat to his grandmother's place in Sibaud. On the first night of one of the most lavish celebrations in Siasi—the legendary wedding of the beautiful Mindamora to Hadji Datu Tunggal, whose wealthy parents showered coins from the balcony of their large house to a crowd of children—Asmawil saw her dance the *pangalay* and decided to run off with her. On the third and final night of the celebrations, above the din of the gongs and the *kulintang* and voices clamoring for her to dance, the motor of the pump boat was heard in the distance.

Nobody knew what it meant. The people were disappointed when she failed to show up. She was out with him on the dark sea, sitting on one of the thwarts of the open boat, in her dancer's suit of lavender silk dotted with sequins. She took off her gold necklace and came to where he was at the stern, steering the tiller. She hung the necklace around his neck and kissed him on the brow and told him not to be afraid, for she was his, here and hereafter.

Yet neither her nearness nor the whiff of her powdered body assured him that she was all his. Half of him was worried about her male relatives, who would be scouring the island when they learned what had happened to her. He knew they would be armed. He turned from her to see if his automatic carbine was still there. It was his only weapon, but it was enough to ward them off, to prevent them from forcibly taking her back. No one, not even her father, could take her away from him now. He swore to himself and to his ancestors that they would only take her away over his dead body. He could not shame himself; but above all, he could not shame her. For he had sworn to her, too, the same vow all true and pure-blooded Tausug made to their lovers, even if he knew there was a tint of that abhorred Samal blood in his veins. What was important in the vow was not the purity of the swearer's blood but his capacity to fulfill the vow, to wear it like his face and skin and not a piece of clothing; he knew that no woman would run off with a man who would not swear by his sacred name and who could not fulfill his vow. This woman, this girl, had complete trust that he was man enough not to run.

He tried to rouse himself from his reverie, but it gave him such immense comfort that he could not shake it from his mind. He lighted another stick of cigarette, and as the smoke made indefinite circles in the air, his mind sank back to that afternoon when Abdul Tungki entered the poop and told him to start going. In turn, Asmawil ordered the crew to release the cables from the bitts at the wharf and in a few minutes the boat, all agog with the raucity of the engine and the bell from the poop, set sail for Sandakan—one day and two nights away. The wooden hull of M/L *Morning Glory* was very light for its size, having been designed for fast sailing by the skilled boat makers of Sibutu Island. Fitted with two ninety-horsepower Yanmar engines, it would use only one engine on a safe regular trip. The second was a standby engine in case the boat ran into naval boats patrolling the boundary between the Philippines and Borneo. Once in a while the second engine was used just to keep it in shape. In the days of smuggling blue-seal cigarettes, naval patrols were more frequent and the slower boats always ran out of luck. They were caught and towed behind a naval boat to Bongao, the nearest port of call from the boundary, where the crew members were imprisoned and the boats impounded; or the merchandise and crew were lost to rapacious pirates, who made guns their primary capital in the lucrative business. The fastest boat was the luckiest, and Asmawil was proud that the *Morning Glory*—a name he had chosen himself because, invariably, it would have sight of its destination in a blaze of glorious sunrise—had never suffered humiliation or loss. *Allah be praised for such a boat,* he would pray in his unconventional way. He would never be a pilot of a slower boat. He would not take too many risks.

In the past he had known fear—the very shape of it, the way it struck him like cold air that, suddenly from nowhere, pierced his skin and stiffened his nipples and entered the hollow of his stomach—and he would experience the loosening of bowels. Often it came in the shape of a heaving sea. What lurked beneath the sudden swell, the mysterious and the unpredictable, what the eyes could not see and the mind could not anticipate, was what he feared more than the broadsides of the patrol boats or the firepower of the pirates. He knew he could always return the compliments with his own firepower, though that was a last resort. The easiest way was to steer away from the course of enemies or outrun them on the high seas. But he could not arm himself against that which he could not anticipate; responding to the unpredictable, when it happened, took a superior intelligence and vast composure. Yet fear of the unknown, rational as it was, was not to be revealed to another man, even to his copilot, who confidently steered the boat windward.

Last night he had no such fear. The weather was good. The cold wind was gentle and caressing. Within the range of his vision were the lights from the fishermen's boats and crystals of foam on the otherwise still surface, and the only sounds were the engine throbbing, almost like the heartbeat of the night itself, and the gentle, incessant vibrations on the railing against which his body was pressed. Not fear, but awe—an awe so sacred that only an act of total surrender could capture its sanctity; to speak of it would only spoil its immediacy and ineffableness. Last night awe had filled his being as he wondered how in their silence the sea and the sky were one. No horizon separated them. Black merged into black. He had the uncanny feeling that if this boat were to sail on indefinitely, it would, on a night like this, be lifted one degree higher to touch the sky's rim. So quiet were the empty spaces, he felt like a solitary earthling on an odyssey between the galaxies. The illusion of the nearness of the constellations to one another made him feel that no distance was far enough for his boat.

He looked toward the stern, and he saw the smokestack emit a steady stream of blackish smoke. There was something about machines, he thought, that made them reassuring companions. They were so predictable, even the most sophisticated—until they conked out or were abused. Then they became dangerous, as if in their weakness or misuse they asserted their superiority and independence.

Many years ago he had thought about going back to school to finish a teacher's degree at the local college. He had quit school to support his wife and children, with only two more years to go. He wondered how different life would have been. Would he have enjoyed teaching children in one of the remote islands like Bulikullul? He knew it would have been a constricting, sedentary life, and the afternoons on a remote island would stretch like one big yawn. But he would have had more time with his family and, certainly, no physical danger at all. For that reason it would have been a less exciting life.

Besides, sailing had always been his life. It was a matter of necessity for him and his father, a boatman who had ferried passengers from Siasi to Hambilan and back. In those days there had been no motorized *vinta*s, and he and his father had to use the sails or, on windless days, paddles. The sails were triangular and old, patched with pieces of clothing that made the sails colorful. When the wind was strong and the sails unfurled, it was smooth sailing. He would sit back at the stern, the paddle held securely in the crook of his leg. One third of the paddle was underwater and served as the rudder of the *vinta*. This way he could daydream during much of the trip, or simply watch the sea birds dive for food on the surface of the water, while his father went around collecting ten *centavos* from each passenger on the boat.

His father went out of business when pump boats became fashionable. But that was many years later. Meanwhile he had grown up, muscular and tall, and the Samal tint of his hair had almost completely disappeared. One summer vacation, when he was big enough to steer the helm, he was taken on as an apprentice pilot with *Sisabros,* the fastest motor launch ever to ply the Siasi-Jolo route. Its famous pilot, Harudji, taught him everything he knew. Most pilots of that time maneuvered their boats in a safe, wide arc, bringing them far beyond the right wing of the wharf. Harudji disdained that kind of maneuver as too time consuming. He would boldly steer his boat directly toward the right wing, running at full speed as if he were going to ram the boat against the cluster of piles. At less than twenty meters he would spin the helm several times around, swerving the bow to a sharp angle and at the same time reducing speed, until the old tire-bumpers on the starboard creaked menacingly against the piles. About the time Asmawil entered college, he had learned this dangerous art and had developed a deep sense of pleasure for what was dangerous.

School bored him. The teachers were unimaginative. What had kept him in school for two years was the opportunity to read stories of high adventure on the sea, of sea captains who were hunters and hunted, of rapacious, mutinous crews, and of uninhabited islands with buried treasures at the end of the globe. The *Pequod* and the *Patna* had haunted him to the point where he saw in each a world more real than his own. When he quit school and found a job as an assistant pilot of a smuggling boat, he had few regrets. He felt he was simply going back in time, repeating the work of his father, going back into the world of his boyhood. It was, he felt, his birthright, his romance with the sea.

He was so absorbed in his thoughts that he did not notice the wind had changed course. He had been drifting for hours, but still no island fringed the horizon. By his reckoning it was nearly noon. The distant water had begun to shimmer in the heat, and under a light breath of wind the sea was like a million fish scales. He went to the kitchen and cooked something for lunch, then went down into the engine room. He noticed the bilge had risen to a dangerous level; it had, in fact, reached the wooden frame on which the engines were mounted. He started the motorized water pump. It began to make a sucking sound.

He went up and examined the bodies. The blood had dried and caked around the wounds and on the floor, and its bad smell assailed his nose. The heat, he thought. He went back into the engine room and, after hesitating a moment, carefully wound a light piece of rope around the ridge of the circular head of one engine. With one vigorous pull the engine thundered in his ears, and his whole body shook with the vibrations of the hull.

Taking the helm, he turned the bow 180 degrees and watched as the compass needle slowly moved east. He was moving opposite the sun's path, against the wind, in the direction that would lead him back to Siasi. He knew that, and he knew that there was no other place for the dead but Siasi, where their families would bury them and avenge them; and he knew, too, on whose head their vengeance would fall. It should not be on his head, but it could well be because they would doubt his story. Vengeance would make them doubt the most naked truth. He was not turning back to Siasi for the sake of the truth. He knew its consequences not only for him, but also for his wife and children. He was turning back because it was the only place for the dead, and the dead needed burial. He was not concerned with decorous, purificatory rites: the bathing of the body, the shaving of the face, the white shroud, the mesmerizing prayers chanted through the night. The rites were for the living who needed distractions because they could not see death in its sheerest simplicity. As for the dead, even those who had made their living from the sea needed one thing only: a place in the bowels of the earth.

The tarpaulin was flapping incessantly on the bow, and the wind was blowing the smell into the poop. Leaving the helm, he went back into the engine room and started the other engine. He knew he had to get back to Siasi before evening, before the smell became unbearable. He thought again of the folks who believed that each dead person was accompanied by forty-four evil spirits. If so, he thought, there should be 396 of them on the boat, and they could gang up on him and hurl him against the engines or drown him in the bilge. It would have been better, he thought, if they did, and it would be the end, rather than this journey of infinite solitude. The thought of these spirits in the engine room made the hair on his nape stand on end. He reached back and slapped his neck three times. He climbed to the deck. He hurried to the poop. And then he realized that there was no one but him, the wind, the sound it made on the tarpaulin and the smell it carried, the engines with their vibrations, and the wavelets in the half-empty glass beside the binnacle.

He knew what he would do when he got back to Siasi. He would tell the story exactly as it happened—no more, no less—exactly as he remembered it. The bare facts would suffice, and they were easier to tell. In less than thirty minutes the authorities would know all they would want to know. But the truth was a different matter. It would not be necessary. It was powerless to bring back the dead anyway.

He would not tell the authorities, unless they wanted some embellishment, how the sharp, metallic sound of the armalite had broken his sleep, how for a moment he had lain frozen, wondering if it was a nightmare, and then how it was followed by another burst of rapid sounds, like a hammer on a nail. He had jumped out of his bunk and entered the poop and, in the dark, had seen a shadow dragging something; then he had asked what it was, and when the shadow had answered, he knew it was his nephew.

Plainly he would tell the authorities that it was his nephew who had killed the men. Why Tadji did it only Tadji knew, and he too was now dead. How could Asmawil know what it would take to kill eight people? Only madness, and he called his nephew insane. Tadji said it was for a reason. Abdul had insulted him, called him *lagak,* glutton, and Asmawil said it must have been only a joke. Tadji insisted that Abdul had meant to insult him; otherwise, why did he do it in a restaurant, where there were many people? Where Sali, Akmad, Ummar, and the others were present; they also laughed when Abdul said Tadji was big because he ate too much and made a great deal of sound like a pig. But if Abdul got what he deserved, what about the others? Because they laughed, too, and they heard the insult; and if they lived, they would talk about his crime. That was how Tadji explained his madness, but it did not explain human madness at all—why there was such a thing in the world. The authorities may accept the explanation as plausible. So Asmawil thought he would simply repeat what Tadji had said. He would add only what he had seen at dawn, that Tadji was counting the money in the attaché case and that it came close to 180,000 *pesos*. He would not tell the authorities, because it was beside the point, that he knew the wife of Tadji had an inordinate fondness for jewels and movies and clothes, and that Tadji was a devoted husband. He would not tell them that when Tadji, with a mysterious smile, had asked him if he wanted some of the money and he had said no, he did not want the money of other people, the smile suddenly changed into a threatening glare. He would not quote Tadji, who said it was not the money of Abdul, but the money of the middlemen. He would not tell them that he did not argue the point because it was dangerous to make a madman see that it was all the same, for it was not his money, and that in silence he called his nephew a pirate. He would ask the authorities to return the money to the middle-men, whose names and the barter merchandise they had ordered Abdul had carefully written down in his notebook.

There was only one thing left for him to tell, and that needed an explanation. He would confess that he killed his nephew, his wife's nephew. He hoped the authorities would be satisfied with an explanation of how he had done it, how he outwitted a big, young man with an armalite, and that they would not ask him, until later in court, to reenact the whole sequence of his crime because it was painful to go through the details once more. Later perhaps, he would be kinder to himself; he would absolve himself of any guilt because it had been necessary to defend himself against a madman. Just for now, he hoped, he would only explain how he had done it, but even that was painful enough because it was shameful and sordid. It was not worthy of him to have done it, but it was necessary to kill a madman while he was off his guard, while he was squatting half-naked over the hole of the toilet, his back facing the door. Why Tadji trusted him after threat-ening to kill him, Asmawil thought, he could not explain. He had attrib-uted it to the mysterious workings of fate because, quite simply, fate did not want him to die that day. It was Tadji's life that had run its full course. But whether it was fate or chance was another matter. Tadji said he would kill him because he knew his uncle would talk, and he suspected that Asmawil wanted part of the money in spite of his denial. He was sparing his life for the time being because he needed his uncle to take him back to Siasi, that as soon as they were near the island his uncle would have to die, too. He told him that in Siasi he would tell the police that they had been robbed by pirates and that his life was spared only because the pirates knew his wife. Asmawil wanted to laugh at this ingenious lie, but it was a madman with an armalite who stood before him, and he was not tempted to wrestle with him for the gun. Tadji told him to keep his eye on the helm while he went to the kitchen to look for something to eat, and he warned Asmawil not to come near or he would shoot him. Asmawil heard no sound of utensils from the kitchen for a long while. He grew excited when the suspicion struck him that Tadji was in fact in the toilet. Knowing that Tadji had the armalite did not deter Asmawil from going to the kitchen for the knife. He had to take the chance to save himself. The long curve of the head of the knife must have caused Tadji enormous pain, he thought, for Tadji had swallowed the smoke of his cigarette and coughed when the knife struck the hollow around his collar bones, and a prolonged snore came from his mouth.

That was the story, not as he would like to tell it to the authorities, but as he remembered it. He would tell the other details, if they were necessary to convince them, but he would rather not. They would ask for the approximate time of the day when it happened, as if a man would slaughter another man at a specific time, like a goat or cow at the slaughterhouse. Goats and cows were killed more mercifully, he thought, with the sharpest blade, like a *kris* or a *barung,* with one's own personal weapon, so that death was swift and there was less pain. On more than one occasion he had seen an *imam*, a religious man, slaughter a goat after a solemn prayer. Perhaps because its meat was to be eaten.

Would the authorities like to know about the weather, too? He would tell them of last night's windless lull, of a world peacefully asleep. But even if the wind and the sea had raged, their fury would have been nothing compared to the madness of last night. Veteran sailors and competent weathermen could tell you when a storm would strike. They knew the places where the waves were always huge the whole year round, and they would tell you to avoid those places. Look for a harbor in the season of the *habagat,* the sailors would say. Sail in April and May when it is *uttarah.* The wind and the sea had their season of peace, as if they had a mind of their own and obeyed a meaningful pattern. No, he decided, the authorities would not ask him about the weather. It was not their duty to know about it. They were not sailors. It was also beside the point. The weather had nothing to do with the madness of man. And he knew the authorities were right.

The sun was down in the west when he got near Sirum, the island before Siganggang, which lay opposite Siasi. Two hours more, he said to himself, but, almost immediately, he remembered he was running on two engines. One hour, he corrected himself.

When he saw the mountain of Siasi rise slowly on the horizon, a sudden vision of his own death gripped him. Turn back, an inner voice told him, turn back. He felt powerless against the lure of the harbor. And he was tired, and the desire to lie down beside his wife in a comfortable bed overpowered his instinct to preserve his life. Besides, where would he go? Out there on the high seas, what would he have? He could not drift forever.

Soon he would run out of oil, and he was sure the weather would change. He would have to find a harbor, a foothold on some land. If it meant facing the avengers of the murdered sailors, so be it. There was a slim chance that they would believe him. But even then, he would have to face the avengers of Tadji. He had not thought of Tadji's brothers when he killed him in self-defense. He knew that self-defense did not exempt him from the stringent law of vengeance. Would it have been better if it were he, instead of Tadji, who was dead? For having outlived Tadji, for having bought a fraction of human time, he knew he had to pay with his own blood, and perhaps the blood of his children, too. While his mind was debating whether he had acted wisely in bringing the dead back to Siasi, the boat moved irrevocably within sight of the island.

In the twilight sky, the tallest landmarks of the island stood above the lights from the squat houses. From the distance, the telecommunications tower was a sharply tapering edifice, without lights ever since its antennas had been struck down by lightning many years before. The church belfry did not look so imposing now as when he was a boy. A very long time ago, he used to sit beneath a camachile tree at angelus, not to listen to the clang of the bell, which did not please him, but to watch the startled doves fly out of their niches when the bell rang and circle uncertainly for a moment about the belfry, like erratic silhouettes in the dusk. The needlelike minarets of the mosque did not seem to soar as high as they did at noon, when their chalky whiteness glinted in the sun. Darkness seemed to dwarf them. The faithful who built them had wanted them to soar beyond the highest pitch of the muezzin's call to prayer, to soar to the bosom of heaven itself. The dome of the mosque was crowned, appropriately, by the ubiquitous symbol of Islam: a star above the crescent moon. Yet the sight of it did not summon religious fervor in his heart, nor images of the tur-baned missionaries who had come to this shore centuries ago, nor the fiery swords of Bedouin sheiks crushing their icon-worshiping enemies. What images it summoned were supplied by the folk belief about fugitive lovers pursued by the armed relatives of the girls. He saw two runaway youths who would consummate their desire and repeat the eternal drama of love and birth. Further into his vision, images of the children of those lovers rose before him like the procession of the future itself—not ghostly faces, but clear, bright, and brown faces, like those of his own children, wearing in their smiles the innocence of those who would not inherit the blight of their parents, as if they were to be the new creatures, running and playing on the primal shore, basking in the maternal warmth of the earth's first morning.

Reviews

■ FICTION

Dirt Music by Tim Winton. New York: Scribner, 2002. 411 pages, cloth $26.

Plenty of writers mistrust the short sentence, except as an occasional breather between long ones. Not Tim Winton. In his early forties, with a career's worth of novels already behind him (*Cloudstreet, That Eye, The Sky,* the Booker-nominated *The Riders*), Winton creates rich characters who work as hard as he does, who won't spare time for a lot of windy introspection unless fate backs them into it. Especially in his salty, frequently very funny dialogue, Winton and his people all sound as if they've got nails in their mouths. When the landscape of his beloved Western Australia carries him away, though, Winton turns lyrical with a sensuous, unsyrupy beauty few other writers can touch. His latest novel, *Dirt Music,* should enhance his small but fervent following in the United States. If it catches on here with anything like the popularity it did in Oz, it could well light up the whole Qantas reservation switchboard.

Dirt Music hitches together several archetypal stories. It's a love triangle that becomes a road novel before evolving into a *Robinson Crusoe*–style desert island idyll. Weaker characters might not have held together such a jerry-built, stubbornly unmanipulative novel, but with Winton we needn't have worried.

Winton introduces us first to Georgina "Georgie" Jutland, an intelligent, bored, fortyish ex-nurse turned "lobster moll." She's falling out of love with her common-law husband, Jim, a lucky fisherman with a violent streak. Along comes Luther Fox, a lonely seafood poacher with bad luck to rival Jim's good, and the fuse is lit for a confrontation made all the more ominous by Winton's reluctance to play favorites among his characters. Plainly, not everybody's going to walk away happy, and we're welcome to wonder whether some will walk away at all.

Winton is juggling a few themes here. Luck and its changeability—or lack of same—come in for a good long look. Solitude, too, its loneliness and its consolations, finds in Winton an observer of uncommon sensitivity. When Luther takes refuge on a tropical atoll, the narration subtly modulates into the second person as if he's talking to himself for want of company.

Winton's also a dab-hand at bereavement both sudden and lingering, a skill that comes in handy for a novel in which recurrent mayhem freights even the shortest vehicular trip with uneasy suspense. His staccato sentences work heartbreakingly well here, slowing down the violence into haunting flashes and distilling the rhythms of grief-racked speech: "I just. Miss. My mum, Jude said between awful gulping sobs."

It's a potent irony of *Dirt Music* that most of the middle-aged adults wax nostalgic for their childhoods, while one or two younger characters have traumas that any sane person would look forward to forgetting as soon as possible. At times this grimness, plus perhaps one or two dream sequences too many, threaten to sandbag the story under a burden of portentousness. Late in the novel, Winton's prose flirts a bit with high-minded murk, too, of which the line "He feels himself within himself" supplies a suitably gluey example.

What redeems *Dirt Music* throughout are Winton's humor, his romantic faith in the power of love to come along and screw up even the most rut-bound lives, his tactile regard for rude, nouny particulars of physical labor and, not least, the majesty of his regard for nature. Just listen to this interlude from Luther's thrillingly described walkabout along the north coast:

> He finds that if you sit still long enough the bush or the sea will produce an event. You wait with trancelike patience until manta rays begin to roll in the shallows or baitfish form like stormclouds along the spit. A beetle big as a golfball will fall from the woven pandanus. A turtle ups periscope in the stillness. A sheet of lightning scours the brainpan.

No wonder they call it Oz.

DAVID KIPEN

Family Matters by Rohinton Mistry. New York: Knopf, 2002. 448 pages, cloth $26.

Written by Rohinton Mistry, who was born in Bombay and has been living in Canada since 1975, *Family Matters* is an impressive and masterful novel. It is sweeping in scope (covering almost five hundred pages), yet intimately detailed in its description of family apartment living in Bombay. The pace was at first ponderous, and I had to remind myself of great Asian films, especially Indian, whose rhythms are slower than the instant hit of Western films. But I soon became caught up in the lives of the wonderful characters in the story.

Nariman Vakeel is a seventy-nine-year-old widower who is stricken with Parkinson's disease and who lives with his two stepchildren—middle-aged spinster Coomey and bachelor Jal—in a once-elegant, seven-room flat. His younger, "blood" daughter, Roxana, lives in a small, two-room apartment with her husband, Yezad, and their two young sons. Nariman breaks an ankle on his daily walk, requiring a full leg cast and bed rest for three weeks. The story is reminiscent of *King Lear*—which Nariman taught as an English professor—as it becomes a saga of "who will take care of Pappa." Torn between familial bonds, religious obligations stemming from their Parsi background, and bitter memories revolving around the death of their mother, the stepchildren (mainly Coomey) conspire to send Pappa in an ambulance to Roxana's already-crowded apartment. Three weeks extend to four months, during which time we learn—memory by memory, in flashback—of Pappa's love affair with Catholic Lucy, his arranged marriage to Yasmin, the widowed mother of Coomey and Jal, and the horrific accident that ended her life. Meanwhile, Roxana's family suffers from lack of space and privacy and from the onset of poverty as Pappa's medical expenses tip their budget over the edge.

How these characters deal with this family obligation is brilliantly drawn. They are alive and passionate, tragic and comic, cruel and compassionate. Yezad's transformation (two times) is profoundly moving, yet finally ironic. It took me into a new world, a new experience of the senses—especially of smells. The odors of bedpans and unwashed bodies and talcum-dusted armpits in the muggy heat of Bombay swelter through this novel like an olfactory mantra. The theme of corruption—personal and political—dances with that of love and goodness, as represented by Nariman's innocent grandson, whose first act of dishonesty is instigated by his desire to make money for his grandfather's medicine.

Mistry's books have won many literary prizes, including the Commonwealth Writers Prize for Best Book and *Los Angeles Times* Book Prize for Fiction. His books have been shortlisted for the Booker, the International IMPAC Dublin Literary Award, and the *Irish Times* International Fiction Prize. I can see why.

JEANNE HOUSTON

Waylaid by Ed Lin. New York: Kaya Press, 2002. 169 pages, paper $12.95.

Waylaid, a terrific first novel by Chinese American writer Ed Lin revolves around a twelve-year-old coming of age in New Jersey in the 1970s, burdened by his virginity and motivated mainly by the pathetic desire to lose it. Taking place in a seedy hotel on the New Jersey shore, it's a heartbreakingly funny set piece in which a working-class immigrant family from Taiwan struggles to make a better life for itself in the bleakest of environments, but can't.

The unnamed narrator has to grow up quickly, and though he's emotionally fragile he hides his vulnerability with a tough-guy posture. He's preternaturally composed for a twelve-year-old, and the book's tone mirrors his "get down to business" attitude. The kid spends his day in the "prison" of the hotel, where he's "Top Dog" manning the front desk. He rents rooms to hookers and johns, lonely old men whose shirts smell like hotel soap, and families whose homes have been repossessed. He cooks his own meals of eggs and Baco Bits, and generally holds his own against the sleaze and sadness of the world.

The universal pain of growing up is pitted against family obligations that are specific to Asian families. Though he rejects his father's traditional values, there is little to fill the void because he has too much work to do, putting holes in the rooms, fixing windows, ticking off items from the to-do list his father has taped to his closet door. But the boy wants to go to college, has higher ambitions:

> "Next year I show you how to use blowtorch and soldering so you can make copper tubing we need for sinks. Very easy."

"All this stuff you're showing me you don't even need to go to college for. Doing this makes me forget everything I learn in school. Doing this makes me stupid. I don't want to work here for the rest of my life."

"You have to have some practical knowledge. You don't want to learn Chinese, you don't want to eat Chinese food, so you can learn how to fix floors."

The parade of colorful customers and their cultural stereotypes would be enough to deflate anyone's dream: when customers make comments to him about Asians, their frame of reference is usually one war or another—Viet Nam, Korea. But the narrator has a snarky sense of humor.

He is not your geeky pocket-protector Asian protagonist. By turns crude, depressing, desperate, and funny, *Waylaid* is a raw and honest portrayal of a boy's transformation to adulthood. Its crude honesty is a cause for celebration, like an Asian American hybrid of *Catcher in the Rye* and *Portnoy's Complaint*.

If the book is autobiographical, Lin has come a long way from the shores of North Jersey. The author holds degrees in mining engineering and journalism from Columbia University. If this novel is an indication of his writing talents, they are prodigious. I can't wait to see what he writes next.

LEZA LOWITZ

Yellow by Don Lee. New York: W. W. Norton & Company, 2001. 255 pages, cloth $22.95.

The stories of *Yellow*, Don Lee's first collection, set in the fictional town of Rosarita Bay, issue from the same literary heartland as Faulkner's Yoknapatawpha County and Sherwood Anderson's Winesburg, Ohio. But these well-crafted takes on American tradition come with a twist: most of their characters are Asian American.

Starting with the book's title, Lee's stories complicate and question. In the title story, yellow is obviously the color of Danny Kim's Asian skin, a fact he spends his life trying to escape. But the word takes on other, equally significant meanings. When, during one of the story's defining moments, a Hispanic boxing opponent calls Danny "yellow" during a match, does the insult refer to Danny's race—or his lack of courage? Or does the color flag Danny's penchant for Midwestern blondes who have that "inherent wheat-field glow"?

Asian by ancestry, the diverse protagonists in *Yellow* lead an ordinary Californian life: they have fish barbecues, go surfing, teach elementary school, and visit Japan as awkward *gaijin*. Their lives outside of work are likely to consist of "one-pot meals and nights alone with videos and errands invented to get out of the house." Friends and lovers loom larger in these stories than parents do, and the past—cultural, familial, or personal—rarely dictates the present.

However, in these stories ancestral inheritance is a powerful vestige: battered against, recovered, surrendered to, and hidden behind. Lee's characters find that the American dream of an endlessly mutable identity—of "colorlessness"—is impossible; in "Lone Night Cantina," Annie Yung's attempts at the American

West are more pitiful because she is so obviously Asian. No matter how much she perfects her "howdy-doody accent," no one will ever mistake her for a cowgirl.

Neither is it possible to go back. Lily Kim's adolescent stint as a "born-again Korean" in "Yellow" doesn't last; when she reappears in "The Possible Husband" as a thirty-nine-year-old artist, her "roots pilgrimage" to Korea is only one of a series of youthful travels, all of which have faded into the distant past.

Yellow pays tribute to the rural roots of American literature while dragging its small-town solidity into a twenty-first-century landscape of transience and marginality. This collection, so American in form and tone, challenges its readers to recognize that its culturally jumbled, post-immigrant content is, by now, more American than apple pie.

LAVONNE LEONG

Unless by Carol Shields. New York: Fourth Estate, 2002. 224 pages, cloth $24.95.

For a shortish novel, Carol Shields's newest, *Unless,* has a few different books inside it. There's the narrator's personal story, that of a hitherto happy woman named Reta whose college-age daughter has inexplicably parked herself on a Toronto sidewalk with a placard strung round her neck reading, simply, "Goodness." There's Reta's professional story, that of a writer attempting a sequel to her only novel, a light summer read called *My Thyme Is Up.* And running parallel to both is a reasonable but angry, often witty meditation on the way society consigns women to its margins.

At a different phase in her career, Shields might have given each of these books a life of its own. Unfortunately, Shields, the author of the Pulitzer-winning novel *The Stone Diaries* and the Orange-winning novel *Larry's Party,* has been fighting cancer. The title of Reta's first novel thus emerges as a bitter joke because the author's time is, if not up, then cruelly in danger of truncation.

Consequently, Shields seems to have elected to give us all three books at once. The result is a novel of questionable cohesiveness but assured intelligence and defiant vivacity. Its stories and themes cross and recross without ever quite braiding, leaving an impression of unforced naturalness that becomes lifelike almost to a fault.

Early on, Reta takes a moment to describe the writing of her friend and mentor, a feminist pioneer whose autobiography she is translating from the French. It's worth quoting this jewel-like passage because it may just be Shields's attempt to preempt the predominantly male critics who would pigeonhole her in some "women fiction" ghetto that insults women in general as much as it insults her in particular:

> She had always claimed that she had little imagination, that she wrote out of the material of her own life, but that she was forever on the lookout for what she called putty. By this she meant the arbitrary, the odd, the ordinary, the mucilage of daily life that cements our genuine moments of being.

Write about life's mucilage, especially from a female perspective, and the literary establishment stamps you as quaint, a miniaturist, or worse. Shields surveys literary history and sees precious few women admitted to the pantheon.

Here's where Reta's daughter, Norah, and her passive panhandling come in. Almost everyone in the book sees Norah's silent renunciation of family and society as a reproach of middle-class life, of the complacency that allows the First World to ignore the sufferings of the Third. But "goodness" isn't just the opposite of evil; it's also the opposite of "greatness"—a laurel customarily withheld from countless female writers.

Seen in this light, Norah's street-corner vigil becomes a stand-in for the predicament of the "good woman writer." Passersby tower over her as they rush past. Some toss her a coin, less often a kind word. And ultimately, in a nicely earned ending that surprises readers without cheating us, everyone around Norah turns out to have the young woman's motives at least partly wrong.

What female writer doesn't know the feeling?

Unless is an odd title for a book, and Shields knows it. It's one of several chapter headings she uses with a rationale that doesn't come completely into focus until near the end, when, with her usual delicacy, she writes:

A life is full of isolated events, but these events, if they are to form a coherent narrative, require odd pieces of language to link them together, little chips of grammar (mostly adverbs or prepositions) that are hard to define, since they are abstractions of location or relative position, words like therefore, else, other, also, thereof, theretofore, instead, otherwise, despite, already, and not yet.

The word *unless* is another of these "chips of grammar," one that must have haunted Shields as she began a novel she couldn't finish unless, of course, her health held out. The novel may not be quite the coherent narrative some of her earlier books are, but none of its three principal strands pulls away so easily that removal would leave a better book behind. Now if only fate would allow Shields to go back to writing her books one at a time.

DAVID KIPEN

Melal: A Novel of the Pacific by Robert Barclay. Honolulu: University of Hawai'i Press, 2002. 300 pages, paper $14.95.

A first novel that left me dazzled, *Melal* is about three generations of a Marshall Island family, their spirit cosmology, and how they have coped with American occupation of the islands and with erosion of their traditional ways of life. The story hinges on one fateful day when two brothers decide to go fishing and camping on the island Tar-Wōj, which is in an American missile range. Once their ancestral home, the island is now off limits to them. Defying the law and their widowed father's concern for their safety, the two brothers set out and have a disastrous encounter with a boatload of American teenagers, who are also fishing. Meanwhile, their father, Rujen, is having one of his worst days ever on Kwajalein

Island, where he works for the American sewage-treatment plant. Due to a series of mishaps and cultural collisions, Rujen, a highly respected Marshallese, discovers serious flaws in his carefully constructed conservatism and what he had perceived as a tolerable level of acceptance by the American community. Shadowing the events of the day are the spirit of the family's dead grandfather (a rebel who never accepted American authority) and a lively cast of modernized gods, demons, and dwarves whose power dramas invisibly determine the course of the day's events for the protagonists. Robert Barclay vividly describes the crowded, slumlike island Ebeye, where young Marshallese commit suicide at an alarming rate, and the push and pull of American jobs and culture on a people who have been relocated and forced into dependence on foreigners. All of the characters—the Marshallese, the members of their spirit world, and even the Americans—are well developed and deeply, sensitively drawn.

LAURA LENT

Caprices by Sabina Murray. Boston: Houghton Mifflin Company, 2002. 210 pages, paper $13.

Caprices is a collection of short stories set in the Philippines, New Guinea, Australia, and Thailand—in jungles, prison camps, and villages with the World War II campaign in the Pacific as historical backdrop. In spare (not stark), richly imaginative prose, Sabina Murray takes us into the minds of men, and some women, struggling to survive under ghastly circumstances. I was especially impressed with the story "Walkabout," whose characters (two brothers) are part Aborigine. An interesting piece, "Position," imagines Amelia Earhart landing on Saipan and chillingly describes the island's citizenry jumping off cliffs—either suicide or prodded by Japanese soldiers. The writing is visceral and, in some passages depicting the landscape, also lyrical. This is hard-hitting, amazing stuff written by a young (34 years old) woman who, with great imaginativeness, has made good use of family stories passed on about World War II.

JEANNE HOUSTON

After the Quake: Stories by Haruki Murakami. Translated by Jay Rubin. New York: Knopf, 2002. 193 pages, cloth $22.

In *After the Quake: Stories,* Haruki Murakami has invented six masterpieces loosely connected by the Kobe earthquake of 1995. In elegant prose, he combines fantasy, surrealism, comedy, and restrained emotion to tell stories of the aftermath of the disastrous quake. My favorites are "Landscape without Flatiron," "Thailand," and "Honey Pie." The first is a beautifully wrought tale of Junko, a rootless young woman who is drawn to an older suicidal artist who routinely builds structures out of driftwood and then sets fire to them on the beach. Their shared intimacy of this ritual is "warming" to Junko's heart even though the artist tells her, "When the fire goes out, you'll start feeling the cold. You'll wake up whether you want to or not."

"Thailand" is the tale of a middle-aged woman doctor specializing in thyroid medicine who takes a vacation in Thailand and learns from a native spiritualist that her unlived life and stoney unforgiveness have created a rock in her gut that, after she dies and is cremated, will be all that is left in her ashes.

"Honey Pie" tells the story of Junpei, an introspective writer, and his strange "ménage à trois" relationship (not sexual) with his best friend Takatsuki, and his wife, Sayoko, with whom he has been in love since college days. After Sayoko and Takatsuki divorce, the narrator remains close to the wife and daughter and finally releases his pent-up yearning by creating a bedtime story for the child that reveals his frustrations and failings.

In these stories, Murakami is a genius at transforming bizarre, inconceivable situations into emotionally powerful stories that explore the longing and withheld expressions of love that imprison man in this absurd creation called modern life.

A joy to read, and knock-out writing.

JEANNE HOUSTON

Letters to Montgomery Clift by Noel Alumit. San Francisco: MacAdam/Cage Publishing, 2002. 247 pages, cloth $25.

Letters to Montgomery Clift is the wrenching story of Bong Bong, a young Filipino boy who is sent to live in Los Angeles with a mean aunt after his parents are beaten in his presence and then disappear during the Marcos regime. The abusive aunt disappears too (much later we find out she was nabbed by immigration authorities) and Bong Bong spends the rest of his childhood shuttling from foster home to foster home. He misses his parents intensely and wonders why they've never come for him, and he escapes into a secret world of one-way correspondence with Montgomery Clift. As he reaches adulthood he gets in touch with Amnesty International and discovers that his father died in prison, but his mother is probably still alive in the Philippines. Meanwhile, he finds out that his foster dad was a money-launderer for the Marcos regime. Bong Bong's self-destructive masochism escalates into cutting, random sex, and a total breakdown that results in a long hospitalization and estrangement from his foster family. As the story ends, Bong Bong finds his mother, starts a relationship with a decent man, and begins to turn his life around. The harrowing story is well-told in the first person. The writing is searing and honest.

LAURA LENT

A Breath of Fresh Air by Amulya Melladi. New York: Ballantine Books, 2002. 224 pages, cloth $23.95.

A Breath of Fresh Air is a crisply plotted story of a modern Indian woman who was exposed to poisonous gas when her philandering army-officer husband forgot to pick her up at the train station on the night of the Bhopal disaster. Anjali breaks deep cultural taboos by divorcing her husband. She remarries a kind math professor and has a child with him, but her child is born with serious physical defects. When her first husband and his new wife are posted in her town, Anjali discovers that she has borne a son damaged by the aftereffects of Bhopal. Her anger is revived, and she is forced to relive her past while her son's health is rapidly deteriorating. The book is an emotional and accessible page-turner. The protagonist describes, with great sensitivity, her evolution from a shallow, materialistic girl to a thoughtful and assertive woman. The quality of the writing leaves it somewhat short of transcendent, but it tells a powerful story.

LAURA LENT

The Character of Rain by Amelie Nothomb. Translated by Timothy Bent. New York: St. Martin's Press, 2002. 176 pages, cloth $19.95.

Elegantly translated from the French by Timothy Bent, *The Character of Rain* is a uniquely conceived self-portrait composed of scenes that evoke laughter, squeamishness, and sheer admiration of the narrator's cleverness. The narrator, whose name is the Japanese character for rain, calls herself "God," "Plant," "the Tube," and "I" during a period (two-and-a-half years) of self-imposed coma beginning at birth. Born in Japan, but of Belgian descent, she suddenly awakens from her vegetative existence "howling with rage" and continues nonstop until her grandmother (visiting from Belgium) feeds her white chocolate. The delectable sweetness gives the narrator her identity: "I" and "me," discovered through pleasure! She insists, "no pleasure without me, no me without pleasure!"

Her two nannies, Nishio-san and Kashima-san, are wonderful characters of opposite nature and class who give the reader insight into Japanese attitudes. A delightful read—satirical, surrealistic, tender, and loving.

JEANNE HOUSTON

A Collection of Beauties at the Height of Their Popularity by Whitney Otto. New York: Random House, 2002. 256 pages, cloth $23.95.

Whitney Otto's *A Collection of Beauties at the Height of Their Popularity* is a visual and literary treat. Illustrated with beautiful reproductions of woodblock prints by eighteenth century Japanese artist Utamaro, the story takes place in San Francisco's North Beach in the early 1980s, and revolves around the lives of patrons of the Youki Singe Tea Room. As Utamaro depicted the Floating World of his time— the pleasure quarters that existed for the pursuit of music, food, sex, fashion, and theater—this novel gives us a world of young people, most of whom do not work at the jobs for which they had been educated, drifting through life without commitment, except to parties (lots of pot, cocaine, heroin, and booze), passion for art and books, and friendship with one another (although betrayal is not unusual). Eulodia Parker, one of the Tea Room devotees, writes of the imagined intimate lives of the circle in her self-styled "pillow book," named after a journal kept by Edo courtesans.

Elegantly composed, in the style of the delicate "inner" sensibility of Japanese women writers of the eighteenth century, this mosaic of finely detailed portraits explores the interconnectedness of the characters' search for love. While the writing is aesthetically pleasing and the structure creative, the thematic range is limited by the self-indulgent values that characterized the floating world of San Francisco's North Beach in the 1980s. Nevertheless, the book is masterfully crafted.

JEANNE HOUSTON

The Vine of Desire by Chitra Banerjee Divakaruni. New York: Doubleday, 2002. 320 pages, cloth $23.95.

Luminous is the word that always comes to mind when I think of Divakaruni's writing. Sequel to *Sister of My Heart* (though it stands alone with no problem), this is a novel about a love triangle gone horribly wrong. Anju's husband can't quell his feelings for his wife's beautiful cousin and best friend, Sudha. When Sudha and her baby daughter come from India to live with them in California after Sudha's difficult divorce, the delicate balance between the three is soon upended, with tragic results. While the internal dynamic of the love triangle and eventual falling-out between all three protagonists is the novel's primary focus, Divakaruni also poignantly portrays the way each wrestles with cultural dislocation and the friction of changing gender roles. They end up with both greater freedoms and opportunities than they might have had if they had remained in India, but they must tackle much greater anomie and loneliness as well.

LAURA LENT

■ POETRY & POETICS

Fusion Kitsch by Hsia Yü. Translated by Steve Bradbury. Massachusetts: Zephyr Press, 2001. 131 pages, cloth, $13.

The title of Taiwanese poet Hsia Yü's first translated poetry collection is quite apt. In fact, what first drew translator Steve Bradbury to her poetry was that it was both "very Chinese and refreshingly cosmopolitan." Hsia Yü, who lives in Paris, apparently doesn't grapple too hard with the problem of cultural identity. She's just as happy among the mysteries of Paris as in the warrens of her native Taipei.

A popular lyricist and author of four books of poetry, Hsia Yü is prolific and hard to pigeonhole. Her avoidance of a lyric or elegiac poetic voice and her refusal to cultivate a signature style make her work unique. But it's her adoption of various "postmodern" techniques,—such as pastiche, montage, and repetition—and her quirky fusion of high philosophy and low culture/kitsch that make her unpredictable. Sometimes she seems to be flying in the face of convention, flaunting her wit and tossing a philosophical wink out to the universe, mocking the seriousness of the enterprise of life. Other times, she's dead serious and probing. It's all material for art. It's all a game, it's all laughable, she seems to say. In "Epithalamion for a Tin of Fish," she takes a traditional marriage poem and serenades sardines in rhyme, perhaps offering a whimsical allegory, perhaps not.

> Lying in its bed of tomato sauce (or is it catsup?)
> Our fish may not quite relish its position;
> But what does the sea know of this, in its deep abyss?
>
> Or the shore, for that matter, no less at sea, as they say.
> 'Tis a tale told in scarlet (or is it cherry red?);
> Whatever—a little silly this matchup;
> Which is to say it is, in point of fact,
> A saucy tale about catsup.

If any influence is evident in her work, it is that of French culture and literature, especially surrealism and impressionism, but to say her influence is global is perhaps more accurate. According to Bradbury, a translator and professor at National Central University in Taiwan, her "Chinese-ness" lies in her preoccupation with the poetic resources of the Chinese language, which she explores with "breathtaking sensuousness."

"Nearly everyone who has written about Hsia Yü's poetry has described her as a feminist poet, a label that has infuriated the author, partly because she chaffs at being reduced to an 'ism' but also because her feminism is problematic at best," Bradbury comments. "She's more concerned with the intersection of flesh/text than with gender or culture." Indeed, Hsia Yü's poems are often deliberately spicy and provocative, like salsa—the title of one of her collections. You can almost taste the vibrancy and piquancy of the language on the page, aided by the subversive freshness of what she chooses as her subjects and concerns. She draws not so much from the basket of traditional cultural motifs (seasons, nature) but from the global hand basket and its universal themes (love, sex, life, death) and how they are captured in language. In *Fusion Kitsch,* she writes:

> When did it all begin
> This bucolic and pan-incestuous atmosphere
> Was it not always there in the selfsame family album
> Lovers fallen to the status of kin
> Animals fallen to the condition of lovers
> Nor let us forget the repressive inclinations
> In the animistic discourse to which
> All romances arrive in the end

Hsia Yü's is a vibrant voice from the edge of the new world, where East and West no longer matter as poetic distinctions.

LEZA LOWITZ

Let Those Who Appear by Shiraishi Kazuko. Translated by Samuel Grolmes and Yumiko Tsumura. New York: New Directions, 2002. 49 pages, paper $12.95.

Shiraishi Kazuko was born in Vancouver, Canada, in 1931. Seven years later, she moved with her family to Japan, where the effects of World War II made a deep impression on her. By the time she was seventeen, her talent as a poet was recognized by Kitasono Katsue, the great pioneering avant-garde poet who led the VOU group of surrealist artists and poets. Later on she became independent of any coterie and in the early 1960s began reading her poetry to the accompaniment of experimental jazz. Shiraishi led a liberated lifestyle, overturning taboos against explicit sexual language and imagery long before the fiction writer Amy Yamada.

In 1973, Shiraishi was a guest writer at the International Writing Program at the University of Iowa. She had already published five books in Japanese, and this experience broadened her view of the world. Indeed, she began to see herself as an international poet. Others saw her this way as well, and she was invited to perform her poetry worldwide. In 1978, New Directions, under Kenneth Rexroth's direction, published Shiraishi's first book of poems in English translation, *Seasons of Sacred Lust.* This new book contains poems from volumes published in Japanese between 1984 and 2000.

To fully appreciate the scope of Shiraishi's art, one must witness her live performances. She continues to experiment by fusing her poetry reading with the sounds of jazz, Ainu music, industrial trash cans, century-old water from an ancient iceberg, and shamisen, and with other media such as photography, video, Flamenco dance, and the butoh dance of Ohno Kazuo. It's not possible to understand Shiraishi's work without hearing her dramatic voice, which can be nearly frightening in its lilting power. However, *Let Those Who Appear,* a modestly thin, long-awaited publication, will give readers a hint of why Mishima Yukio said that she was the best poet in Japan, and Allen Ginsberg echoed this statement.

The breadth of Shiraishi's themes range from the warning of the dangers of technology, especially cloning (the opening poem "I and I"), the ironical criticism of virtual reality, to environmental concerns ("A Bear of the Human Family"), national identity ("The Laughing Cricket"), government control ("The Donkey Speculates"), the narrowing of the human heart ("The Residents of the Cocoon"), and sex ("Woodpecker"), just to name a few.

The translation team of Samuel Gromes and Yumiko Tsumura and New Directions have given us an accurate and respectable English rendering of the poems of Shiraishi Kazuko, one of the great artist-performer poets of our time.

TAYLOR MIGNON

Poems of the Goat by Chuya Nakahara. Translated by Ry Beville. Richmond: American Book Company, 2002. 77 pages, paper $15 (2500 ¥).

It's often been said that translation is a labor of love. Nowhere is this more true than with the translation of poetry, which, as Baudelaire said, is a kind of universal translation, since poets translate the language of the universe—mountains, rivers, trees—into the language of humanity. So why do some writers get translated and others (better, more deserving) remain obscure? It's a question Ry Beville asked himself seven years ago. This book is his answer.

In 1995, the Virginia native was studying literature at Nanzan University in Nagoya and attempting to translate Ōe Kenzaburō when a professor shared with him an article he'd written about poet Nakahara Chuya. The article quoted a line from "The Cicada": *"Utsura-utsura to boku wa suru."* The rhythm and music of the line resonated with Beville, who had always admired the more "musical" poets of the last century like Yeats, Auden, and Frost. Beville went right to the bookstore and bought a collection of Chuya's poems in Japanese; there was no English version on the shelves.

Beville felt it was almost a "crime" that a poet as extraordinary as Nakahara Chuya—not to mention as admired among the Japanese—was not only unavailable in English, but also unknown to many Western scholars of Japanese literature. "I undertook this project in part to correct that balance, if only a little. But more importantly, I wanted to let the English-speaking world know that there is a poet with a style as diverse and accomplished as some of the greatest modern writers in the West."

Chuya was born in 1907 in Yuda Onsen, Yamaguchi, to an army doctor and his wife. Though the family moved to Hiroshima and Kanazawa, they returned to Yamaguchi in 1914. As a child, Chuya wrote poetry and *tanka*, but as a teenager he discovered alcohol, and the distance between him and his family grew. He was sent away to a fancy private school in Kyoto, where he was introduced to dadaism and French symbolism, and fell in love with an older woman actress. In 1926, he met the critic Kobayashi Hideo and devoted himself to poetry, leaving his family and small town far behind. The rising influence of European culture was felt against the growing tide of imperialism and nationalism. In 1931, Chuya enrolled in Tokyo University's foreign-language school and began compiling *Poems of the Goat,* but the manuscript had a hard time finding publication. By age twenty-six, he had entered into an arranged marriage and was publishing poetry and writing lyrics. Living a somewhat profligate life in the city, Chuya was the prodigal son and did not return home for his father's funeral—something almost unheard of at the time. *Poems of the Goat* was the only book he saw published during his lifetime. In 1938, at the age of thirty, he died of tuberculosis. Shortly before that, he gave another manuscript, *Poems of Bygone Days,* to Kobayashi. It was published posthumously, and Beville is now translating it.

Chuya matured in a time of immense social change, with industrialism, modernism, and the dark shadow of war impacting the social and political landscape. His poems are elegies to lost times and places, sad celebrations of the shabby underbelly of existence, both inner and outer: the circus, a hangover, a sigh, cigarettes, a lover. And yet Chuya's poems are suffused with an innocent resignation, much like the pastoral goat after which they are named: a gentle animal often used in sacrifice. In "Poem of the Sheep," he writes:

I'll embrace my fate at the hour of my death!
I'll lift this little chin of mine—lift it to the heavens.
Only now do I understand that this death
Is the consequence of all I was unable to feel.
Yes, I'll embrace my fate!
And then I'll finally know how it all feels!

For whatever reason, certain poets become spokespersons for their age. Chuya seems to have won that role, perhaps by being both in and of his era. A bohemian by nature, he was deeply impassioned about life yet somehow alienated from the world, wavering between hopeful nostalgia and existential crisis. When he is writing about nature, it's always through the prism of a damaged, and human, psyche. Here is an example from "The Twilight of This Spring Day":

Little by little, the temple in the pasture reddens
The wheel of the horse-drawn wagon is dripping oil
If I make some kind of remark at this historical moment
I'm heckled—heckled by the sky and mountains

For years, Chuya has been a lasting cultural icon whose poetry has appealed to a wide range of Japanese readers. His somewhat wild persona—drinking and smashing up places, even landing in jail—has also led to a certain mystique. But it's always the music that sticks with people.

"When I describe Chuya (to Americans at least), I liken him to Frost," Beville says. Chuya's appeal also cut across generations. "I am constantly amazed," Beville says, "to find people in their twenties—and these are not literary nerds but hip youth out in the bars and on the streets—who love Chuya. With such a large and diverse readership, Chuya certainly seems like the kind of poet that Westerners interested in the Japanese—not simply Japanese literature—should read." Now, thanks to Beville, they can.

LEZA LOWITZ

■LITERATURE & CULTURE

The Complete Idiot's Guide to Understanding Buddhism by Gary Gach. Indianapolis: Alpha Books, 2002. 408 pages, paper $18.95.

This is a book with a whole lot going for it, if you can get past the title. Who wants to admit to being an idiot, even if it is tongue-in-cheek? In truth, the journey into a Buddhist perspective starts even before you open the book. Seen from a Buddhist point of view, you could translate idiot mind into Beginner's Mind and consider yourself ready to become an adept. And you couldn't ask for a better guide than Gary Gach, who has forty years of Buddhist study and an impressive career as an author-editor-translator to his credit. Open the pages, and you're immediately in the company of a quiet monk, learned philosopher, and stand-up comic. This is exactly the combination of reverence, erudition, and zany humor you'll need on the path to enlightenment—even if you have no intention of ever getting there.

For the scholarly, Gach gives a thorough overview of Buddhist history, teachings, ceremonies, and practices, starting with who Buddha was and what Buddhism stands for and leading to a clear and engaging discussion of the Four Noble Truths and the Eightfold Paths that underlie Buddhist thought. Gach also explains the major schools of Buddhism, such as Vipassana, Zen, Pure Land, and Tibetan, covering the rules and beliefs of each. He explores the growth and development of American Buddhism, which is a very unique animal of its own. If you still need clarification, there's "Glossary of Silence" in the back of the book.

For those seeking more practical guidance, Gach dispenses advice on how to meditate (even at meals) and do yoga, what to eat, how to find the right spiritual teacher and/or community, where to go for pilgrimages and retreats, and countless other tips. For the artists among us, there are lively sections on Buddhist cinema, haiku, art, the tea ceremony, calligraphy, music (from Yoko Ono to John Cage), science (chaos theory, holistic medicine, psychology), and interfaith connections. Finally, there's useful information on how to bring the teachings outward, such as how to take right action about the environment, how to balance spirituality and materialism, how to be a better listener, how to have a more compassionate relationship with others and yourself, and how to care for the dying.

The text is extremely readable and engaging, and the layout and design keep the mounds of information from being overwhelming. Sidebars, sketches, and boxes ("Leaves from the Bodhi Tree" and "Hear and Now") go easy on the eye and brain. It's like a college seminar on Buddhism distilled into Cliff's Notes. Before you know it, you'll be halfway through the book and down the path.

Here's a sample, "The Ultimate Relationship," of how Gach interweaves Buddhist thought and theory into everyday situations with compassion, creativity, and humor:

> The Buddha said, "Just as the elephant's footprint is the biggest footprint on the jungle floor, death is the biggest teacher." Indeed, our relationship to death includes all other relationships. Consider, for example, how sex once again pokes its head at us when we consider death. You probably wouldn't think of death as part of "the facts of life" (although people whisper about death and shield children from it as if it *were* sex). The fact is if it weren't for sex, we might not ever face the mystery of death.
>
> Consider, for a minute, that if we still reproduced by cell division, one cell dividing into two, two into four, and so on, instead of Harry meeting Sally and later bringing up baby Harry Jr., we'd have Billy becoming Bill *and* Lee. Mary-Lou would become Mary and Lou. And so on for everyone. (Imagine what weird family reunions all *that* would make.)
>
> Now, if we looked at death as part of life's sexual embrace, we might not grieve so badly when one thing becomes another. A caterpillar becomes a but-

terfly. (Does the caterpillar die?) An infant becomes a teenager. (Does the infant die?) A breadwinner becomes a retiree. A strong parent becomes a frail being, lying in a bed, sipping nourishment through an I.V. tube. Who dies? It's the story of anyone.

Buddhism provides various skilful means for all life's relationships. As death is inherent in all our life transformations, all our relationships, we come now to the ultimate question: how can we face our lives if we don't face our deaths? The Zen answer is, "Die before you die." Then, when your time comes, you'll be ready. (Nobody said it's easy.)

The author's winning style is totally contagious. Like his previous book, *What Book?! Buddha Poems from Beat to Hiphop,* which won the American Book Award, this is a celebration of Buddhism past, present, and future. With incredible breadth and depth, *The Complete Idiot's Guide to Understanding Buddhism* makes Buddhism more accessible, but it also makes it meaningful and fun. After reading it, you'll feel more like a genius than an idiot, but with your new sense of lightness and detachment, you'll realize how little these labels matter.

LEZA LOWITZ

The Nick of Time: Essays on Haiku Aesthetics by Paul O. Williams. Edited by Lee Gurga and Michael Dylan Welch. Foster City: Press Here Books, 2001. 112 pages, paper $12.

What is a haiku, really? How do we know one when we see it? Are English-language haiku less authentic than Japanese haiku? And how do we know if a haiku is bad? These questions are answered—and more are raised—in *The Nick of Time,* an important and delightful new volume of sixteen essays by master haiku poet Paul O. Williams. These ruminations on the art, craft, and love of haiku will go a long way towards advancing the discussion of what constitutes this ancient and revitalized form.

As trends and debates about haiku come and go, the time is right for a classic that takes the middle road. This is the book. Its title is from this quotation from Thoreau: "In any weather, in any hour of the day or night, I have been anxious to improve the nick of time, and notch it on my stick too; to stand on the meeting of two eternities, the past and future, which is precisely the present moment."

Which is precisely where haiku reside. In "The Burst of Haiku," Williams writes,

Haiku discovers the unusual and significant in daily life, shows it is not quotidian but often startling. Things happen. Haiku sees the astounding nature of these things, or the universality, or the fineness of quality there, or the uniqueness and significance...We deal with wonders on a daily basis. It's a matter of astonishment, and haiku tends to point out that surprise of discovery we feel when we perceive these new dimensions.

Williams has lived and breathed haiku for nearly half a century, first being asked about the form by a student in 1964. A charter member of the Haiku Poets of Northern California, he was also the founder and editor of its journal, *Woodnotes*. In 1999, he became the president of the Haiku Society of America, and he's published three books of haiku. The essays in *Nick of Time* reflect a deep concern with haiku's language, image, form, style, and, most of all, authenticity. With the publication of the book, more readers can share in Williams's lifetime of discoveries.

"While a passion surely exists in haiku, it is often reserved or at least understated," Williams writes; yet he could never be accused of lacking passion, which is like a strong undercurrent guiding the river here. It's especially evident in "Tontoism in American Haiku," in which he states that many English haiku sound like Tonto conversing with the Lone Ranger because they lack articles—which Japanese doesn't have—and are "vaguely campy." Citing such examples as "old man/digs potatoes/in rain," Williams doesn't suffer haiku fools lightly. "An Apology for Bird Track Haiku" is a deliciously ironic manifesto about pseudo-Zen nature writing, and the Nabokovian dialogues between doppelgangers Alphonse and Gaston—"Baloney Haiku" and "Haiku Reviewing"—are sure to make writers and reviewers reevaluate their methods and standards, laughing at themselves along the way. *Nick of Time* also has a brilliant comparison of haiku and fiction, Williams being a haiku writer who's authored eight books of science fiction.

These essays were published in such haiku journals as *Modern Haiku, Ko, Frogpond, Dragonfly,* and *Woodnotes* over the past thirty years. Editors Lee Gurga and Michael Dylan Welch—themselves master haikuists and tireless promoters of haiku in America—have performed an incredible service by putting all this writing in one place. (The book can be ordered from Welch by writing him at P.O. Box 333a, Redmond, Washington, 98703-3339.) Anyone writing haiku, thinking about writing haiku, or thinking about haiku will be enriched by having this indispensable, lyrical manual.

LEZA LOWITZ

About the Contributors

John Balcom received his doctorate in Chinese and comparative literature from Washington University at St. Louis. He is an associate professor in the graduate school of translation and interpretation at Monterey Institute of International Studies.

Nick Bozanic lives in Honolulu with his wife and two sons, Gabriel and Isaiah. His most recent book is *This Once: Poems 1976–1996;* selections from his new work-in-progress, *Trust,* are forthcoming in an anthology to celebrate the thirtieth anniversary of Anhinga Press.

Steve Bradbury teaches poetry and children's literature at National Central University in Taiwan. His first volume of translation is *Fusion Kitsch: Poems from the Chinese of Hsia Yü* (Zephyr Press, 2001).

Lynda Chanwai-Earle was born in London and spent a large part of her childhood in Papua New Guinea. She is a television journalist and writer and has studied fine arts and drama at Auckland University. In addition to *Ka-Shue (Letters Home),* published in 1998 by The Women's Play Press, she has published a book of poetry, *Honeypants* (Auckland University Press, 1994).

Chen Kehua was born in Hualian, on the east coast of Taiwan, in 1961. A trained ophthalmologist, he is also a prolific writer of fiction, essays, plays, film criticism, and song lyrics. He is the author of many books of poetry, the most recent of which is *I Picked Up a Skull* (2002).

Chen Li was born in 1954 and raised in Hualian, Taiwan. He began writing poetry in the 1970s under the influence of modernism, and in the 1980s turned to social and political themes. By the 1990s, his work explored a wide range of subjects and styles, combining formal and linguistic experiments with concern for indigenous cultures and the formation of a new Taiwanese identity. In collaboration with his wife, literary critic Zhang Fenling, he has translated the work of a large number of Latin American and East European poets, including Neruda and Szymborska.

Chu Van (1921–1994) wrote such well-known novels as *Sea Storm, Saline Soil,* and *Shooting Star.* His fiction collections include *When the Phoenixes Return, The Singing Behind a Curtain,* and *The Pearl of Lovesickness.* He was the chairman of the Literature and Art Association of Nam Dinh Province in Viet Nam and the director of the province's Culture Service.

Gavan Daws has written eleven books and a stage play. His work has taken him back and forth between the United States and Australia, with stints in Europe and Asia. His documentary films have won awards internationally; his songs have been performed at the Hollywood Bowl and the Waikīkī Shell and in clubs from San Francisco to Greenwich Village. He lives in Honolulu. More of Iona Contemporary Dance Theatre can be seen at www.iona360.com.

Du Shisan is the pen name of Huang Renhe, a novelist, essayist, visual and performance artist, and poet. Born in 1950 in Zhushan, Nantou Province, Taiwan, he has won awards from the *China Times* and *Epoch Poetry Quarterly.*

Sergio Goes was born in Brazil and has been living in the United States for the past thirteen years. His photography has been exhibited at the Whitney Museum of American Art, the London Biennial, The Contemporary Museum, the Honolulu Academy of Arts, and elsewhere. *Black Picket Fence,* his feature-length documentary, received a Special Jury Award in HBO's Documentary Feature Competition, as well as awards from the Brooklyn International Film Festival.

Jeanne Wakatsuki Houston is the coauthor with her husband, novelist James Houston, of *Farewell to Manzanar,* based on her family's imprisonment in the Japanese-American internment camps of World War II. She also coauthored the Viet Nam memoir *Don't Cry, It's Only Thunder* and authored a book of personal essays, *Beyond Manzanar.* She recently completed her first novel, *Firehorse Woman.*

S. Yumiko Hulvey is an associate professor of Japanese language and literature and the associate dean for academic affairs of the College of Liberal Arts and Sciences at the University of Florida. She has published translations of narratives by Enchi Fumiko and critical articles on women writers of classical and modern Japan. Forthcoming is *Sacred Rites in Moonlight: Ben no Naishi Nikki,* her translation of the thirteenth-century poetic memoir by a woman who served at the court of Go-Fukakusa.

Hung Hung is a poet, translator, and theater and film director living in Taipei, Taiwan. He was born in 1964 and received a bachelor's degree in drama from the National Institute of Art.

Jian Zhengzhen was born in 1950 in Taipei County, Taiwan. He received his doctorate in English literature and comparative literature from the University of Texas at Austin. He has served as chief editor of *Epoch Poetry Quarterly* and chairperson of the department of foreign languages and literature at National Zhongxing University. Author of many books of literary criticism, he has also published seven volumes of poetry; an eighth, *Paradise Lost*, is forthcoming.

Nick Kaldis is an assistant professor of German, Russian, and East Asian languages at the State University of New York at Binghamton, where he teaches Chinese language, literature, and film. He has published articles on Lu Xun's poetry and on the cinema of Taiwan and China.

Wayne Karlin is a novelist and the coeditor, with Le Minh Khue and Ho Anh Thai, of Curbstone Press's Voices from Viet Nam series.

David Kipen is the book critic for the *San Francisco Chronicle,* a member of the board of directors of the National Book Critics Circle, and a steering committee member of the California Studies Association. He was also the senior editor of *Buzz*, a Los Angeles magazine.

Kurahashi Yumiko was born in Shikoku, Japan, in 1935. She has been a major force in experimental Japanese fiction since the early 1960s. An English translation of her short stories, *The Woman with the Flying Head and Other Stories* (M.E. Sharpe, 1997), contains works from her *Cruel Fairy Tales for Adults* (1984) and *Path of Dreams* (1989). The three stories in this issue are from *Path of Dreams.*

Laura Lent is a coordinator of book selection for the San Francisco public library system, a member of the collection development committee of the Public Library Association, and president of the documentary film group Pelican Pictures.

Lavonne Leong is a freelance writer and editor living in Honolulu. She received her doctorate from Oxford University.

Li Jinwen was born in Gaoxiong County, Taiwan, in 1965. He has worked as a journalist and is now an editor for Tomorrow Studio. He has published two books of poetry and has won many awards.

Ling Yu was born in Taipei County, Taiwan, in 1952. She received a baccalaureate in Chinese from National Taiwan University and a master's degree in East Asian languages and literatures from the University of Wisconsin at Madison. She began writing poetry in the early 1980s, when she became editor of *Modern Poetry Quarterly* in Taiwan, and has published four volumes of poetry. She was a visiting scholar at Harvard University in 1991 and 1992. She currently teaches at the National Yilan Institute of Technology.

Andrea Lingenfelter received her doctorate in Asian languages and literature from the University of Washington in Seattle in 1998. She has translated the poetry of Zhai Yongming and Fu Tianlin and the novels *Farewell My Concubine* and *The Last Princess of Manchuria*. She composed the film subtitles for *Temptress Moon* and is now translating *Candy,* the first novel by the Shanghai writer Mian Mian.

Liu Kexiang is from Taizhong County in central Taiwan. Born in 1957, he received a baccalaureate in journalism from Chinese Culture University and now works as an editor for the *China Times*. During the early 1980s, his political poems were widely read on college campuses. Since then, he has devoted himself to nature writing. He has published three books of poetry and three prose collections.

Leza Lowitz is *Mānoa*'s reviews editor and corresponding editor for Japan. She has written two books of poetry and translated eight books from the Japanese. Her newest book, written with Shogo Oketani, is about the Japanese ideogram.

Luo Fu is the pen name of Mo Luofu, who was born in Henyang, Hunan Province, China, in 1928. He joined the military during the Sino-Japanese War (1937–1945) and moved to Taiwan in 1949. In 1954, he founded the Epoch Poetry Society with Zhang Mo and Ya Xian, serving as the editor of *Epoch Poetry Quarterly* for many years. In 1973, he retired from the navy as a commander and graduated with a degree in English from Tamkang University. His poetry has been widely influential in both Taiwan and China.

Luo Ying was born in 1940, and has been writing poetry since the mid-1950s. A graduate of the Women's Teachers College in Taipei, she worked as an educator for more than a decade. A member of the Epoch Poetry Society, she has published two books of poetry, *Catcher of the Clouds* (1983) and *One-Half Joy* (1987). She currently lives in South Africa where she writes full time.

Luo Zhicheng was born in Taipei in 1955 and graduated from the department of philosophy of National Taiwan University. After working as an editor for the *China Times*, he studied at the University of Wisconsin at Madison, where he earned a master's degree in East Asian studies. Active in Taiwanese media, including television and advertising, he is the publisher of the travel magazine *To Go* and an instructor at Soochow University. He has published five books of poetry, two books of prose, a volume of critical essays, and various translations.

Paul Manfredi is an assistant professor of Chinese at Pacific Lutheran University in Tacoma, Washington. His research interests include modern Chinese poetry and visual culture.

Pat Matsueda is the managing editor of *Mānoa* and the author of two small books of poetry. She met Darlaine Māhealani Dudoit around 1989 and worked with her for several years, becoming a friend. The poem in this issue was written after reading an article on Dudoit's life and the events leading to her death in August 2002; written by Tanya Bricking, the article remains unpublished.

Taylor Mignon has translations, poems, and articles in *Atlanta Review, Japan Times, Prairie Schooner,* and the anthology *Faces in the Crowds: A Tokyo International Anthology*. A book of his cotranslations of *senryu* by Gengoro is forthcoming from Hokuseido Press.

Alberto Milián is an attorney and journalist living in Miami, Florida.

Monaneng was born into the Paiwan tribe in Daren Township, Taizhong County, Taiwan. Owing to malnutrition as a child and to years of hard labor, he lost his sight. Today he works as a masseur in Taipei and writes poems about the island's indigenous people and the blind.

Nam Son is a translator who lives in Ha Noi, Viet Nam.

Ryan T. Scott Nance received his master's degree in English literature from Columbia University and is a poet and translator.

Nguyen Ngoc Tu was born in 1976 in Ca Mau Province, Viet Nam, and works in the Ca Mau Association of Literature and Arts. In 2000, her first collection of short stories, *The Inextinguishable Light,* received first prize from The Youth Publishing House in Ho Chi Minh City.

Nguyen Qui Duc is the author of *Where the Ashes Are: The Odyssey of a Vietnamese Family* (Addison-Wesley, 1994) and the editor (with John Balaban) of *Vietnam: A Traveler's Literary Companion* (Whereabouts Press, 1995). He has translated fiction and poetry by many Vietnamese writers; his latest translation is *The Time Tree: Poems by Huu Thinh* (Curbstone Press, 2003). He is the host of *Pacific Time,* a national public radio program on Asia and Asian American affairs.

 Simon Patton was born in Melbourne, Australia, in 1961. He works as a literary translator and coedits the China poetry domain of the Poetry International Web (http://china.poetryinternational.org) with the mainland Chinese poet Yu Jian. He was an artist in residence at the Taipei International Artists Village in Taiwan.

Ricardo Pau-Llosa has written five books of poetry. His latest, *The Mastery Impulse,* was published by Carnegie Mellon University Press (2003).

Phan Thi Vang Anh was born in 1968 in Ha Noi, Viet Nam, into a family of writers: her mother, Vu Thi Thuong, was a short-story writer, and her father, Che Lan Vien, was one of the great Vietnamese poets of the twentieth century. She has published the fiction collections *When One Is Young* and *The Fair.* She lives in Ho Chi Minh City and works for The Youth Publishing House.

Phan Trieu Hai emerged in the early 1990s as one of the most talented young writers of Viet Nam. He has published several collections of short stories, including *Starting Out, The Boy on the Roof,* and *Going to School,* a travel memoir of the year he attended the Iowa Writer's Workshop. He lives in Ho Chi Minh City.

Hu Qian is a doctoral student at the University of Texas at Dallas. He has translated several books and papers on translation and interpretation.

 Shang Qin is the pen name of Luo Yan, also known as Luo Ma. Born in Hong County, Sichuan Province, China, in 1930, he now lives in suburban Taipei, Taiwan. He was forced to serve in the Nationalist military until 1968, and from 1969 to 1971 he attended the International Writing Program at the University of Iowa. The first poet in Taiwan to be profoundly influenced by surrealism, he has published four books of poetry in Chinese; collections of his works have also appeared in English, French, and Swedish.

 Arthur Sze is the author of *The Silk Dragon: Translations from the Chinese* (Copper Canyon Press, 2001), which received the 2002 Western States Book Award, and *The Redshifting Web: Poems 1970–1998* (Copper Canyon Press, 1998).

Anthony L. Tan was born in 1947 and is a native of Siasi, Sulu, an archipelago of the Philippines that lies southwest of Mindanao and northeast of Borneo. He attended Ateneo de Zamboanga in Zamboanga City and Silliman University in Dumaguete City. A professor at the Mindanao State University-Iligan Institute of Technology in Iligan City, he is the author of two books of poetry, *Badjao Cemetery and Other Poems* and *Poems for Muddas.*

Stephan Torre has been published widely in the U.S. and Canada. His last book, *Man Living on a Side Creek* (1994), won New York University's Bobst Award; and a new book, *Iron Fever* (2003), was published by Lost Horse Press. He lives in the northeastern California Great Basin, and works as a counselor and mediator.

Keith Waldrop teaches at Brown University, and is coeditor of the small press Burning Deck. His *Silhouette of the Bridge* received the American Award for Poetry for 1997.

Walis Nokan is a member of the Pai-Peinox group of the aboriginal Atayal tribe in Taiwan. He graduated from Taizhong Teachers College and teaches at Freedom Elementary School in his hometown, Heping Village, in central Taizhong County. Born in 1961, he started writing poetry at the age of sixteen and has been the editor of *Hunter Culture,* a journal dedicated to Taiwanese aboriginal culture. Active at the Research Center for Taiwanese Aboriginal Humanities, he has published two books of poems and written essays, cultural critiques, journalistic pieces, and fiction. His Chinese name is Wu Junjie.

Wu Sheng is the pen name of Wu Shengxiong, who was born in 1944 in Xizhou, Zhanghua County, in central Taiwan. In 1980, he attended the International Writing Program at the University of Iowa. He teaches biology at Xizhou Junior High School, works on his family farm, and is an essayist and a nativist poet known for his depictions of rural Taiwan.

Xu Huizhi is the pen name of Xu Youji, who was born in 1966 in Taoyuan in northern Taiwan. He has been editor of the *China Evening Express* and chief editor of the literary supplement of *Liberty Times.* He is now chief editor of *Unitas,* a leading literary journal, and has published many books of poems and prose.

Xue Di is the author of *An Ordinary Day, Circumstances, Heart into Soil, Flames, Trembling,* and *Dream Talk.* He is a two-time recipient of the Hellman-Hammett grant and a fellow in Brown University's Freedom to Write Program in Providence, Rhode Island.

Yang Mu is the pen name of Wang Ching-hsien, a leading essayist, prolific editor, and highly respected literary scholar who publishes in both Chinese and English. Born in Hualian in 1940, he has published thirteen books of original poetry in Chinese and his poems have been translated into English and German.

Ya Xian is the pen name of Wang Qinglin, a venerated poet, scholar, and editor. Born in He'nan Province in 1932, he continues to influence poets in Taiwan with work written in the 1950s and 1960s.

Michelle Yeh is a professor in the department of East Asian languages and cultures at the University of California at Davis. Her most recent publications are *Essays on Modern Chinese Poetry* (1998); *No Trace of the Gardener: Poems of Yang Mu* (1998), cotranslated with Lawrence R. Smith; *From the Margin: An Alternative Tradition of Modern Chinese Poetry* (2000); and *Frontier Taiwan: An Anthology of Modern Chinese Poetry* (2001), coedited with N.G.D. Malmqvist.

Hsia Yü was born in Taiwan in 1956 but now divides her time between Paris and Taipei, making a living as a lyricist and translator. She is the author of four volumes of poetry, most recently *Salsa* (1999).

KYOTO JOURNAL

www.kampo.co.jp/kyoto-journal/

KYOTO JOURNAL: 4 issues + 1 bookzine: $50   Pay by credit card   Email: kyotojournal@gol.com